A History of Women's Lives in Liverpool

A History of Women's Lives in Liverpool

Gill Rossini

PEN & SWORD HISTORY
AN IMPRINT OF PEN & SWORD BOOKS LTD
YORKSHIRE – PHILADELPHIA

First published in Great Britain in 2019 by
Pen & Sword History
An imprint of
Pen & Sword Books Ltd
Yorkshire – Philadelphia

Copyright © Gill Rossini, 2019

ISBN 9781526718099

The right of Gill Rossini to be identified as Author of this work has been asserted by him in accordance with the Copyright, Designs and Patents Act 1988.

A CIP catalogue record for this book is
available from the British Library.

All rights reserved. No part of this book may be reproduced or transmitted in any form or by any means, electronic or mechanical including photocopying, recording or by any information storage and retrieval system, without permission from the Publisher in writing.

Printed and bound in England by TJ International Ltd, Padstow, Cornwall

Pen & Sword Books Limited incorporates the imprints of Atlas, Archaeology, Aviation, Discovery, Family History, Fiction, History, Maritime, Military, Military Classics, Politics, Select, Transport, True Crime, Air World, Frontline Publishing, Leo Cooper, Remember When, Seaforth Publishing, The Praetorian Press, Wharncliffe Local History, Wharncliffe Transport, Wharncliffe True Crime and White Owl.

For a complete list of Pen & Sword titles please contact

PEN & SWORD BOOKS LIMITED
47 Church Street, Barnsley, South Yorkshire, S70 2AS, England
E-mail: enquiries@pen-and-sword.co.uk
Website: www.pen-and-sword.co.uk

Or

PEN AND SWORD BOOKS
1950 Lawrence Rd, Havertown, PA 19083, USA
E-mail: Uspen-and-sword@casematepublishers.com
Website: www.penandswordbooks.com

Dedication

This book is dedicated to all the women of Liverpool, but especially my very own Liverpool Woman, my beloved spouse, Lynn Carter.

Contents

Dedication		v
Acknowledgements		viii
List of Illustrations		ix
Introduction		xv
Chapter One	At Home	1
Chapter Two	Health and Welfare	19
Chapter Three	Toil and Trouble: Women at Work	39
Chapter Four	'Sagging Off with a Sprowser in Me Pocket': Education	88
Chapter Five	Mixing With the Woollybacks: Liverpool Women and Leisure	102
Chapter Six	'An Extraordinary Diversity of Races': Women on the Move	127
Chapter Seven	'We'll have no wet nellies here!': Activism and Public Life	141
Chapter Eight	Postscript: 1945–1950	164
Historical Sources		168
Bibliography		171
Websites		178
Index		180

Acknowledgements

This project has been an historical quest, of course, but it is also a community, and a family, venture. My first guided tour of Liverpool, years ago, in the expert care of my Liverpudlian partner, Lynn, was an eye-opener. She showed me empty spaces and painted vivid word pictures of what had been there, and took me to see all the suburbs, city centre sights, and hundreds of buildings. We crossed the water and saw Liverpool's 'cousins', Birkenhead, New Brighton and Wallasey. She answered my hundreds of questions about the city and its people with care and quite often, that unique local humour. She does a fantastic line in Scouse lingo! She and her family, both those still local to Liverpool and others now living abroad, gave me insights I could never have found any other way. The Liverpool museums, libraries and archives have a wealth of information at their fingertips and are unstintingly generous in their sharing of it, and local resources such as newspapers contain stories forgotten for many years until recently. Sources of national importance, such as the Census Enumerator's Returns, offer personal insights into the households, occupations, neighbourhoods and even opinions of those listed – but there is no substitute for the personal, and thank you is never enough.

2018 was my thirtieth anniversary as an adult education lecturer, and the historian I am today is partly the result of the wonderful students I have had the company of over those years. Their lively minds, questioning approach to the past, and support for each other, culminating in the most amazing and professional projects worthy of any library shelf, have been, and remain, an inspiration.

To all of the above, I offer my deepest respect and gratitude.

List of Illustrations

Cover Illustration: Group photograph of staff outside the Central Café, Liverpool, c.1928–30

Map taken from vintage atlas, 1910, depicting Liverpool from Sefton Park to Waterloo, also Birkenhead, New Brighton, Seacombe and Rock Ferry. Title of atlas or publisher not known. Author's own collection.   xix

Sunlight Household Hints Booklet, c.1900. Author's own collection.   4

Two well dressed ladies walking down Summer Seat, Vauxhall, c.1910. Vintage postcard, captioned 'Liverpool cottages on old slum area.' Photographer not identified. Author's own collection.   9

A group of poor girls waiting to collect a charitable hot pot for their families on Christmas day. Illustration from an article in the Harmsworth Magazine, c.1900. Author's own collection.   14

'In Memoriam' card (front and interior views) for Susannah Howard, died 28 October 1877. Printed by Walsh and Sons, 407 Scotland Road, Liverpool. Author's own collection.   21

Photographic illustration of Liverpool Infirmary. Illustration from a book, title not known. c.1900. Author's own collection.   23

Photographic postcard of the Jenny Lind Ward, c.1905. Captioned 'Jenny Lind Ward, Royal Southern Hospital, Liverpool.' Manufacturer not identified. Author's own collection.   25

Agnes Jones. Portrait from a Victorian magazine (title unknown). Verified PDF download with permissions from www.istockphoto.com/gb.   31

Group photograph of staff outside the Central Café, Liverpool, c.1928–30. Probably professionally photographed but photographer not known. Mounted on board. Author's own collection.   39

Unidentified woman in maid's uniform, c.1915–1920. Portrait photograph in postcard format by De Freyne, 1A Lorton, Street, Liverpool. Author's own collection.   41

Young woman delivering milk by the pail in Liverpool, with her pet goose in attendance. Captioned: 'The Goose Step in Liverpool.' Vintage newspaper clipping, title of publication unknown. Author's own collection.   44

Stripping tobacco at the Copes Tobacco factory. Illustration from the English Illustrated Magazine, 1892, Vol 9, page 306. Author's own collection.   45

Making Cavendish at the Copes Tobacco Factory. Illustration from the English Illustrated Magazine, 1892, Vol 9, page 303. Author's own collection.   46

Making cigars at the Copes Tobacco factory. Illustration from the English Illustrated Magazine, 1892, Vol 9, page 305. Author's own collection.   48

The Ogdens Colossal Tobacco Factory, West Derby Road, Everton. Advertisement on cutting from Illustrated London News, February? 1902 (date obscured). Author's own collection.   49

Advertising card for Johnson's Dye Works, Liverpool, c.1900. Postcard style format, from the Grano Series manufactured by The Photocrom Co. Ltd., London. Author's own collection.   51

LIST OF ILLUSTRATIONS   xi

View of Bold Street, c.1906. Photographic postcard
captioned 'Bold Street, Liverpool'. Manufacturer not
identified. Author's own collection.   57

Postcard of sketch of the Reilly Building, University
of Liverpool. Captioned 'Woman's Union' and below
'The University of Liverpool'. Printed and sold to
raise money for the University Appeal to raise one
million pounds. Manufacturer not known.
Author's own collection.   58

D. Carter's wool and drapery shop, Bishop Road,
Anfield, with proprietor standing outside, c.1950.
Personal snapshot style photograph. Reproduced with
kind permission of Ms Lynn Carter.   59

Advertisement, Employment Bureau for Educated
Women, 1934. Clipping from a magazine or directory,
title and publisher not known. Author's own collection.   60

Front cover of instructional book Pitmans'
Shorthand or Phonography. Published by
Isaac Pitman and Sons, London, 1891.   72

Miss Phyllis Lovell putting a group of First World
War women volunteers through their drill, in Liverpool.
Vintage newspaper cutting, c.1914–15, newspaper
unknown. Author's own collection.   77

Two snapshot style photographs of WRNS
(Women's Royal Naval Service) at Greenbank gardens,
annotated on the reverse. Author's own collection.   84

Two snapshot style photographs of Greenbank House,
1944. Annotated on the reverse. Author's own collection.   86

Advertisement for the 'Dolly Varden' folding doll's
house, manufactured by Meccano Ltd. of Liverpool.
From a magazine or catalogue, title unknown.
Author's own collection.   89

A group of Liverpool school girls dressed as
'Pierrettes' c.1925. Vintage postcard. Photographer
not identified. Reproduced with kind permission of
Ms Lynn Carter. 90

Photographic illustration of the University College
(later Liverpool University) illustration from a book,
title not known. c.1900. Author's own collection. 92

Postcard of sketch of the Reilly Building, University of
Liverpool. Captioned 'Woman's Union' and below 'The
University of Liverpool'. Printed and sold to raise money
for the University Appeal to raise one million pounds.
Manufacturer not known. Author's own collection. 94

A church army worker, 1921. Postcard style portrait
photograph by The Parisian Studios, 27, Church Street,
Liverpool. Author's own collection. 100

The palm house, Sefton Park, Vintage postcard, c.1906,
captioned 'Sefton Park Liverpool.' Identified on rear as
'The British Mirror Series: holds the mirror up to nature.'
Author's own collection. 103

New Brighton, The Wirral, photographic postcard
captioned 'New Brighton Ferry.' c.1906. Manufactured
by P&Co Ltd. Author's own collection. 104

New Brighton, The Wirral, postcard photograph
captioned 'The Sands, New Brighton.' c.1908.
No manufacturer identified. Author's own collection. 105

Young Liverpool woman posing outside a tent on the
Wirral, possibly Meols, on a weekend away camping.
Personal snapshot photograph, c.1937. Reproduced
with kind permission of Ms Lynn Carter. 112

Photographic view of Ranelagh Street, Liverpool city
centre. Illustration from a book, title not known. c.1900.
Author's own collection. 115

Women playing crown green bowls, 1920s. Vintage
postcard captioned 'Bowling Green, Muirhead
Gardens, West Derby.' Manufacturer not known.
Author's own collection. 117

The May Queen for Bootle, 1912. Portrait photograph
in postcard format captioned 'Bootle May Queen, 1912.'
Photographer not identified. Author's own collection 119

Woman dressed in crinoline style dress, 1860s.
Photograph by W. Keith, 25 Hardman Street, Liverpool.
Carte de Visite (CDV) style photograph on card.
Author's own collection. 120

Young woman dressed in high Victorian fashion,
c.1874–5. Photograph by Daniel Jones, Bold Street,
Liverpool. CDV photograph on card. Author's own
collection. 121

Edith Johnson, photographed August 1886. Taken at
Medrington Studio, Bold Street. CDV photograph
on board. Author's own collection. 121

Woman dressed in fashion of c.1885. Taken at the
studio of S.D. Kruger, 139 Park Road, Liverpool.
CDV photograph on card. Author's own collection. 122

A young woman dressed in the fashions of c.1885,
and a mature woman in simpler, practical attire.
Photographed by Rattray, 120 Bold Street, Liverpool.
CDV photograph on card. Author's own collection. 122

Young woman dressed in winter fashions for c.1894–5.
Taken at Barrauds Ltd, 92, Bold Street, Liverpool.
Studio portrait on board. Author's own collection. 123

Young woman in the fashion of c.1895–8, with her
baby and her clerical husband. Photograph by Brown,
Barnes and Bell, 31 Bold Street, Liverpool. Studio
portrait photograph on board. Author's own collection. 123

Young woman dressed in fashion from c.1912 with
velvet hat. Studio portrait photograph printed on paper,
in card mount. Photographer: Cottier Cubbin,
175 London Road, Liverpool. Author's own collection.   124

Young woman in everyday costume of c.1915.
Studio portrait printed on postcard, by Lahanc,
145 Walton Road, Liverpool. Author's own collection.   124

M. Murray, portrait photograph Dated April 1920.
Produced in postcard format by Reginald Mobbs,
Greenbank Road, Liverpool.   125

Dora Davenport in her first evening gown, studio
portrait, dated 22 February 1935. Printed on a
postcard, photographer's stamp present on rear
but smudged and unreadable. Reproduced with kind
permission of her daughter.   125

Three young Liverpool women in their off-the-peg
practical business clothes, c.1945–6. Personal snapshot
style photograph. Reproduced with kind permission of
Ms Lynn Carter.   126

Photographic view of the Landing Stage, Liverpool.
Captioned 'Liverpool Landing Stage – R.M.S 'Ionian'
and S.S. 'Canopic'. Illustration from a book, title not
known. c.1900. Author's own collection.   128

Dora Davenport: Studio portrait, c.1939. Studio and
photographer unknown. Mounted on board.
Reproduced with kind permission of her daughter.   166

Introduction

The Diversity of Liverpool

The story of Liverpool's women is one of diversity. By definition, 'diversity' also encompasses different points of view, different ideas, but also different people; any history of a place or a group of individuals cannot be honest or balanced unless it presents both sides of situation – the affluent and the poor, for example, or the law abiding and the miscreants, the locally born and the 'incomer'. Women of many nationalities and backgrounds have come to Liverpool. Some stayed, and made their home here, embedding the culture of their place of birth, religion, and family influence in the city, bringing skills and vibrancy with them. Others merely passed through, taking with them fleeting impressions of the port on their ongoing journey to their overseas destination. Still more stayed for a short time, or indefinitely, meaning to move on but for some reason, unable to do so. To these women we must of course add those born in Liverpool, steeped in its evolving culture, many of whom stayed to build their families there, while other Liverpool-born women grew up there and moved away, 'exporting' their Liverpudlian heritage, education, and vibrancy, to all parts of Britain and the globe.

This is primarily a women's history, but context must be acknowledged – where husbands, fathers, supporters, lovers, and other men have been important in a woman's life, or instrumental in the welfare of Liverpool's women and girls, they have received fair treatment. To do any other would isolate the women from those they loved, their support networks, or the challenges they faced. The women between 1850 and 1950 may have grown up in, and been conditioned by, a patriarchy, but they were still the mothers, sisters, daughters, wives and carers for men and boys, many of whom they loved dearly and that love was reciprocated; some men were also loyal supporters of change and reform.

Thus, this narrative aims to tell a rounded story of the women of Liverpool, in order to give the truest account of this aspect of the city's history. In this port through which millions of people passed as migrants, perhaps staying only a matter of days, the demographics are complex, yet all the women – itinerant workers, migrants, the 'born and bred', the leisure traveller, social campaigner, politician, the vulnerable, the sex worker, and the tourist – all had an impact on the city and its history in some way. The tide of people ebbed and flowed just like the seas the city overlooks, sometimes glittering and basking in the sunshine of success, and at other times, struggling with the effluent of hard times.

This is the story of all those women.

A Portrait of Liverpool in c.1850

In 1851, Liverpool was a focus of trade and commerce, rather than manufacturing, something that was to influence opportunities for women and girls in the city until the turn of the twentieth century. As such it was a town (it was not granted city status, by Queen Victoria, until 1880) that reached outwards across the world, but was also increasingly renowned as an importer of products and raw materials to all parts of Britain. Merchants from East India, the Americas, and the West Indies knew the city well, and most of the employment was in service trades, such as dock work, unloading cargo and taking it to warehouse or onwards to be processed – sugar, salt and soap, for example. Ship building was on a decline, although ship repairs remained a useful source of revenue for the city. From 1800 to 1850, the population of the centre of Liverpool had grown rapidly, but even more rapidly (a growth rate of up to eighty per cent) in the new suburbs of Toxteth, Kirkdale, and Everton. By the 1840s, Liverpool's population density was a staggering 140,000

INTRODUCTION xvii

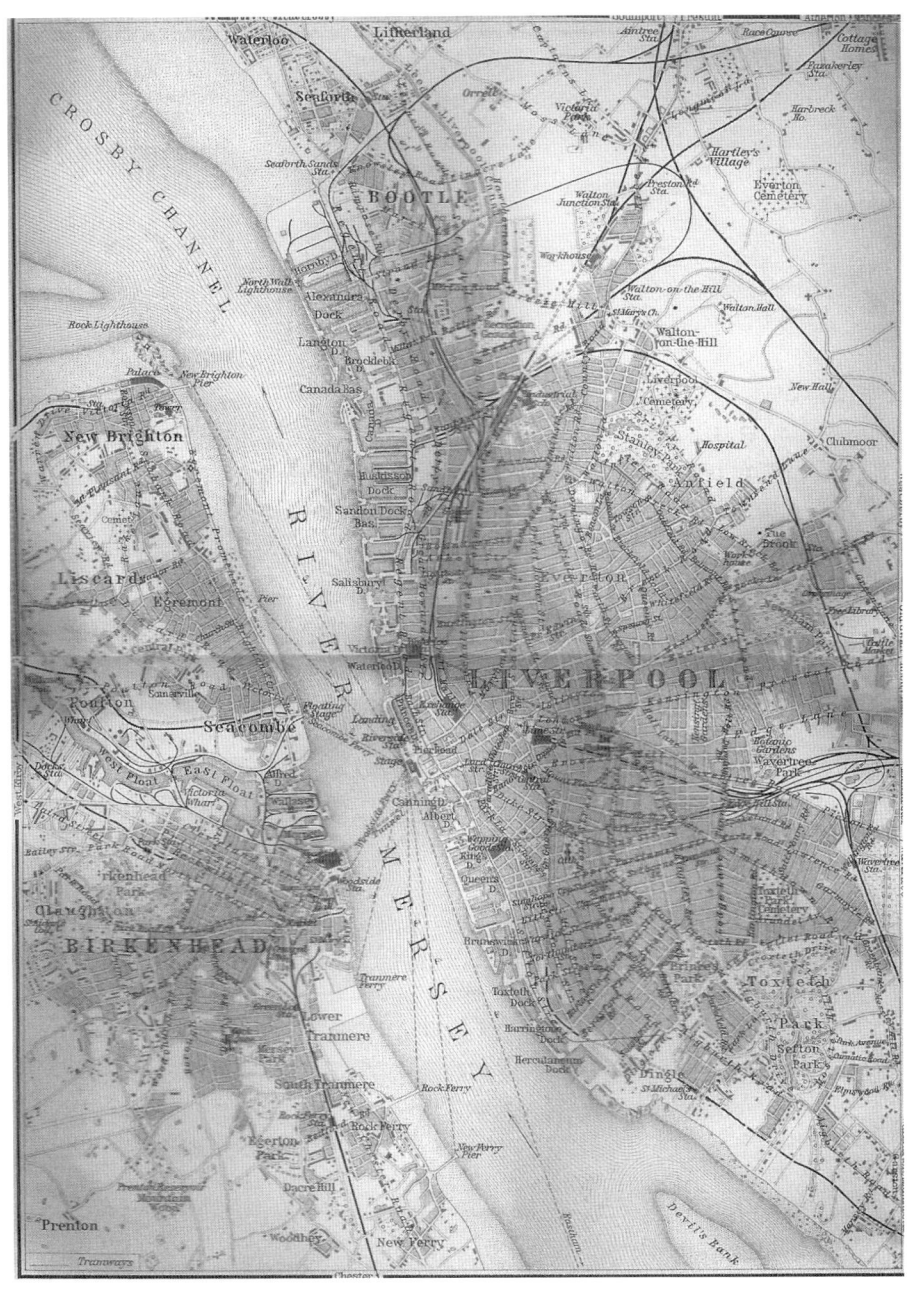

Map of Liverpool in 1910, from Sefton Park in the South to Waterloo in the North. Also shows the River Mersey, Birkenhead, New Brighton, Seacombe and Rock Ferry.

persons per square mile, more than Leeds, Manchester or even London. In districts such as Vauxhall and Exchange it was even higher, mainly due to their being the foci of immigrants after they disembarked. Lace Street had only 4 sq yd per inhabitant, and consisted of a high proportion of Irish immigrants. In the vicinity of Tithebarn Street and Great Crosshall Street, conditions were no better, with densely packed court dwellings.

Everton was originally a village which had its own historical population and a few more affluent Liverpool residents who built mansions there to take advantage of the space and fresh air – it was engulfed as terraced housing developments spread from the north docklands area and up the hill, and by 1851 its population of agricultural workers had become largely a thing of the past. Allerton and Wavertree still retained a rural lifestyle and had numerous agricultural workers listed on the 1851 census, and working farms as late as the 1870s; here, rich industrialists and merchants built their country homes, such as Allerton Towers, and Wavertree Hall. Meanwhile, the high class housing vacated by the merchants in streets such as Duke Street became cramped and overcrowded boarding houses, and played a part in the Asiatic cholera outbreak of 1849, to which hundreds of people fell victim. Bootle, Walton and Litherland gradually changed as the 'carriage people' with their affluent lifestyles and numerous servants moved in, to enjoy less polluted air and better environment, yet Aintree and Childwall actually lost population in the nineteenth century as people – mainly adult females – from the villages were drawn to the centre of the city for work. In 1851, Childwall looks to be a rural idyll, with cottages, numerous farms and the Hall, with Alderman and Mrs Molyneux in residence on the night of the census, as are eleven servants. The seven female domestic servants include three housemaids, one cook, a kitchen maid, and the farming man's wife – only one, 17-year-old Margaret Webster, was born in Childwall, with the others coming from Shropshire, Cheshire and Lancashire. Even on the edges of Liverpool, incomers were having an impact. In fact, by 1851, approximately half of the population of Liverpool was born outside Lancashire.

Liverpool's status as a prominent port also encouraged faster population growth than in inland cities and towns, a factor common to large coastal trading settlements in England.

Any woman out doing her daily shopping in 1850, especially in areas close to the docks, would have been mixing with a wonderfully diverse and cosmopolitan range of people. Liverpool had become the leading emigration port in Europe with 159,840 passengers alone sailing to North America in a trade worth a million pounds in that one year. She may have passed by emigrants speaking any one of a huge range of languages, from Swedish to Polish, Russian, Gaelic, German, Norwegian, Yiddish and many more. There would also be the mariners from all over the world, speaking languages from South East Asia, Southern Europe and the Baltic ports. Emigrant families would be wandering the streets during the day, the women no doubt tired and overwrought if they had children to watch out for, or a baby to carry; their belongings would be in bags, bundles or parcels, and their clothes may, to our local woman, look unusual, even exotic. She may have witnessed them being targeted by local conners or 'runners', who snatched their few precious belongings and held them to ransom. These hundreds of thousands of migrants, who were crammed into boarding houses perhaps for anything from one to ten nights before moving on, were a part of the city's history for a brief moment, but in the larger picture created a diversity that helped to give Liverpool its unique 'personality'.

These were the people who passed through Liverpool on their long journey to a new life far away. What of our local woman? Once she had finished her errands, what sort of home would she return to?

> Liverpool, with all its commerce, wealth, and grandeur yet treats its workers with the same barbarity. A full fifth of the population, more than 45,000 human beings, live in narrow, dark, damp, badly-ventilated cellar dwellings, of which there are 7,862 in the city. Besides these cellar dwellings there are 2,270 courts, small spaces built up

on all four sides and having but one entrance, a narrow, covered passage-way, the whole ordinarily very dirty and inhabited exclusively by proletarians.

So wrote Friedrich Engels in 1845. Poor housing, nutrition and everyday healthcare contributed to the spread of disease – Engels estimated in 1844 that approximately eight per cent of the population of Liverpool perished from 'the fever' on an annual basis. He continued:

In Liverpool, in 1840, the average longevity of the upper-classes, gentry, professional men, etc., was thirty-five years; that of the business men and better-placed handicraftsmen, twenty-two years; and that of the operatives, day-labourers, and serviceable class in general, but fifteen years. The Parliamentary reports contain a mass of similar facts ... epidemics in Manchester and Liverpool are three times more fatal than in country districts; that affections of the nervous system are quintupled, and stomach troubles trebled, while deaths from affections of the lungs in cities are to those in the country as 2½ to 1. Fatal cases of smallpox, measles, scarlet fever, and whooping cough, among small children, are four times more frequent; those of water on the brain are trebled, and convulsions ten times more frequent.

Well into the 1860s, these and other illnesses such as typhus, cholera, croup, pulmonary disease, various types of fever, diarrhoea, and smallpox, claimed many thousands of lives. Our Liverpool woman would add to these risks the perils of childbirth, and the high infant mortality of the times. She would have consoled neighbours and relatives who lost children, and may well have been consoled in turn when she had her own child bereavement.

By 1851, districts such as that around the well known Scotland 'Scottie' Road were already known for their overcrowded and inferior living conditions. In 1842 the Building Act (Liverpool) was passed, and reinforced in 1846. By 1850, a campaign to reform the appalling living conditions in parts of Liverpool began. The Liverpool corporation gained some powers to control what dwellings were built, in an effort to restrict the construction of badly constructed and insanitary 'court' dwellings, and also had powers to inspect lodging houses. Seven years after Engels' damning summary of poverty in the city, Liverpool's first Medical Officer of Health was appointed, Dr William Henry Duncan.

Liverpool continued to receive a bad press, however – in 1853, Nathaniel Hawthorne, the American Consul in Liverpool, used to walk the city taking note of what he saw. Readers were shocked and appalled by what he had witnessed. Of Liverpool he wrote:

> at every two or three steps, a gin shop, and also filthy in clothes and person, ragged, pale often afflicted with humors [sic]; women, nursing their babies at dirty bosoms ... groups stand and sit talking together, around the door steps, or in the descent of a cellar; often a quarrel is going on in one group, for which the next group cares little or nothing. Sometimes, a decent woman may be seen sewing or knitting at the entrance of her poor dwelling, a glance into which shows dismal poverty...[he goes on to say] the anomalous aspect of cleanly dressed and healthy looking young women, whom one sometimes sees talking together in the street – evidently residing in some contiguous house ... in a more reputable street, respectably dressed women going into an ale and spirit-vault, evidently to drink there.

This is the picture of Liverpool that outsiders saw, an overcrowded, muddled, unclean, port, peopled with uncouth women and struggling in its attempts to create a better environment for its residents. As the chapters in this book show, the women of Liverpool were much more diverse, intelligent, interesting and vibrant than Hawthorne gave them credit for.

A word about the Scouse 'lingo'

'Scouse' as a colloquial way of expressing oneself is thought to be a hybrid dialect and vocabulary unique to Liverpool, and according to Scouse expert Tony Crowley (see bibliography), it takes words from as many as thirty-two languages including English; just a few examples are Cornish, Danish, Hindi, Polari (originally used by mariners), Manx, Welsh, Romani, Spanish, Italian and Turkish – a language as diverse as the population of Liverpool itself. Crowley entitles the language 'Liverpool English' rather than 'Scouse'. It was a dialect and vocabulary only infrequently used by the middle classes of Liverpool – one woman who grew up in West Derby told the author she distinguishes between 'Scousers' and 'Liverpudlians' when it comes to mode of speaking and the phrases and words used, a distinction her mother had impressed upon her. In this narrative, I have used some Scouse words and phrases to give character and uniqueness to the story, and where necessary, have included explanations of words or phrases used. It is, after all, a 'lingo' that is regarded with great affection in the city itself, and is recognised internationally. Scouse has changed somewhat over time and has variations between areas within Liverpool too, and if you are familiar with it yourself, you may well use slight variations to the words I have chosen to highlight.

CHAPTER ONE

At Home

Courtship and Marriage

In the nineteenth century, for a woman not to marry was regarded as strange, even freakish, yet early marriage was suggested by the Central Relief Society of Liverpool as a cause of poverty. W. Grisewood, who wrote a milestone series of articles for the *Liverpool Mercury* in the 1890s, interviewed a teenage couple who had married aged 18 and 17. They came from precarious backgrounds – the husband's parents were dead, and the wife had to leave home because of an unkind stepmother. Essentially, this young couple only had each other for every kind of support, from emotional to financial. Their furniture comprised a three-legged table, a couple of old chairs, a dirty mattress (but no bedstead or bed clothes) and a few items of crockery. On a weekly basis, the husband was working as a parcel carrier for a few hours, earning up to 10*s*; his wife was a fish or fruit hawker. Their rent was 7*s* 6*d* per week. (*Liverpool Mercury*, 19 August 1899) Once the first baby came along, followed no doubt by more, their place in the poverty trap would be irretrievable. Working-class people were urged to wait until they were solvent before marrying, but financial security was unattainable for most, and they married anyway, especially if a baby was already on the way.

Decades later, the advantages of later marriage did seem to go hand-in-hand with a better income. The 1934 Social Survey of

Merseyside compared two areas with differing socio-economic profiles and studied the age at marriage in them. In Exchange, 40.7 per cent of women aged 20–24 were married, whereas in comfortably off West Derby, only eighteen per cent of women in that age group were married. Even the way in which women met their future husbands was different according to class. Middle-class women tended to meet their spouses in private clubs, such as tennis or golf clubs, in a relatively controlled environment where, mixing only with their peers, they were more likely to make a suitable match. Working-class young women in fact had more freedom to mix, and a popular way to circulate in safety, with a large number of young men and women, was 'The Rack' – promenading and socialising with one's friends, and eyeing up the opposite sex. The Rack took place every Sunday morning at Sefton Park, while Queen's Drive was a somewhat more suburban setting for promenading. On a summer's morning one could happily sit on the grass with male friends, chat and laugh, while one's better-off female counterparts would walk past apparently with disdain at the largely innocent but socially infra dig proceedings, perhaps secretly envious at the ease with which these young women could enjoy the company of men. However the match was made, the vast majority of women during this period were married in a place of worship.

'You're as black as the cobs of hell!': Keeping Clean and Tidy, and the 'Rituals of Respectability'

Before the Liverpudlian housewife did anything for herself, she had a home to clean. Standing outside a terraced house in a street such as those in Anfield or Old Swan (two examples among many), the first thing a visitor would notice would be the well-washed door, and a doorstep buffed to a colour varying from white through to brown using a 'Donkey Stone' – a block of compressed stone manufactured for the purpose. 'Step dashing' – scrubbing up the doorstep till it was immaculately clean – was also an essential cleaning task, and ground-floor window sills received the same treatment. In the front parlour window would be hanging either summer or winter curtains, and the heavy cotton lace curtain was kept sparkling white with bleach. The front lower-storey bricks were washed to remove the sooty coating from coal fires and pollution, and the pavement was also scrubbed.

Such 'rituals of respectability' were not aligned with class or monetary status. They were almost exclusively a marker for, or test of, moral status and hierarchy. The woman with the cleanest step, crispest lace curtains, best scrubbed table, and most spotless laundry in the street, was superior to her neighbours, no matter how poor they were. One woman in her nineties, originally from Birkenhead but who had lived in Liverpool since 1956, told the author: 'They can take away all your money, you can be as poor as anything, but they can never take away your self-respect' – this in reference to standards in the home. Even the suffrage movement regularly made references to the 'respectability' of their cause, as it was a concept that would be familiar to women from all classes. It was almost exclusively the domain of females to keep this aura of family and home respectability intact, a responsibility that some women would have relished, and others found a suffocating and intolerable burden. Others would have ignored it completely, and struck out to live, work, and love in their own unique way.

The *Sunlight Household Hints* booklet (see page 4) was issued as a free gift by Lever Brothers, the Wirral company and manufacturers of the Sunlight Soap bars, and offers insights into common household and family care challenges that home makers today could never imagine. Coal fires, especially in a poorly constructed or unswept chimney, deposited a layer of soot over everything, so there are suggestions for cleaning 'smoke-blackened' books and whitening discoloured ceilings. If there is a chimney fire, newspaper soaked in water and placed in the grate is the remedy. Cucumber peel can repel cockroach infestations, while cloves deter house flies. A quick way to heat a room is to put several bricks in the oven, leave them till they are hot, and then using a cloth to hold them, place the hot bricks in the parts of the room you want heated – somewhat reminiscent of

Sunlight Household Hints booklet, published by Wirral company Lever Brothers in c.1900. A promotional give-away, the booklet was crammed with useful tips for all those who had to help keep house and look after a family.

the later concept of storage heaters. A small piece of soap left in furniture will deter insects. In between wash days, the housewife had to ensure her flat iron did not rust, so she is advised to rub her iron over with warm grease and wrap it in brown paper, while powdered bathbrick rubbed over the flat of the iron would keep it smooth while actually using it on fabrics. Should you be so slovenly as to allow an earthenware teapot to go mouldy inside, use a strong solution of borax to clean it. And so the advice rolls on, through every kind of material, furniture, tableware, metal and leather, and there were no machines or devices to ease the physical drudgery. Clothes were still laundered by hand, furniture vigorously polished, hearths cleaned and belongings mended and cared for. It is little wonder that women expected their eldest daughters to help out at home.

Homemaking work, housework, housewifery – however it is labelled – is unpaid, and always has been. As the Women's Industrial Council (WIC) wrote in their 1915 report 'Married Women's Work', a case study that included Liverpool women:

> woman's fundamental work – her work as wife and mother, nurse and homemaker – is and always has been, unpaid – in cash. The result is inevitable. In a commercial age work which is unremunerated and a worker who is unpaid are alike of small value and little esteemed … with the consequence that all work done by women and all wage-earning women are paid at a lower rate than would be the case if their work were not cheapened.
>
> (Married Women's Work, p. 106)

This is the stark reason why no matter how 'respectable' a clean home was, as the women themselves would admit, its value was only moral and personal.

Housing

Of the poor housing found across Liverpool, often the worst and least sanitary were court houses. In layout, there would normally be a 'day room' on the ground floor, with one bedroom each on the first floor and second floor. The dark, unventilated and flood-prone cellar below the property was used for washing, storage, or rubbish; each of the four spaces may have housed a separate family if the property had been sub-let. Cellar dwellings were some of the very cheapest accommodation and consequently attracted the near-destitute. These courts often lacked adequate daylight, were impossible to keep clean, and lacked privacy, but amazingly, many families lived in them with remarkable stoicism.

In 1878, newly ordained curate Herbert Dale conducted numerous social visits to court dwellings in the North Liverpool parish of St Mathias, and reported on a Mrs MacClelland and her three surviving children, who lived in Court 26, Porter Street ('first door on the left'). He was moved by her plight:

> Her husband and two children died of smallpox. She takes in a little washing, has a small sickly baby. Barbara is in Mr Howells, and the boy in Miss Muller's school. Clothes are short. But the children seem willing schoolgoers, but depressed and quiet.

A search of the 1871 census reveals the McClelland (note alternative spelling) family in less stressful times. Here, our woman in distress is called Mary, born 1832, and at the time was still married to Patrick, a Scottish mariner. She had five children – Catherine (17), Kenneth (11), Mary (6), Barbara (3), and 8-month-old Roderick. The vast majority of her neighbours are Irish, mostly in family groups, but on Porter Street, there are several lodging houses accommodating Irish dock workers. An overview of the basic family history resources does not reveal a straightforward picture as to what happened to Mary's family next. Patrick seems to disappear, and there is no death registration for him in England and Wales. Certainly his absence, and the deaths of some of her children, would have worsened Mary's impoverished circumstances, and although we tend to think Victorians could just brush off child death, it is highly likely that these traumatic events would have added to the low mood witnessed in her surviving children. As we do not know why Patrick departed the family, either through death, work, or desertion, it is impossible to say if the sickly baby is his. Suffice it to say that Mary and her remaining family were struggling to survive with any semblance of good spirits.

Others were quick to condemn the women who ran the homes in question for their state. Hugh Shimmin, a writer of acerbic sketches he claimed were taken from direct observation, was merciless in 1862:

> the wife has such a poor perception of her duty that she does not even know how to take care of her home ... [she is] given up to filth, and nurses her children in it ... the man is driven to drink and he and his wife quarrel – the children are neglected, morally and physically.

Shimmin went on to predict that these neglected children would take the wrong path in life, and end up in court in St George's Hall, be they male or female, and laid the fault firmly at the feet of their mother, ignoring other social and economic factors.

Although many courts were demolished after the 1846 Sanitary Act, some did continue to be occupied well into the twentieth century, such as those in the area of Scotland Road. As late as 1934, the stigma of living in the courts clung to the remaining residents like the soot and smog they fought against daily; Pat O'Mara wrote, 'The customary domestic procedure of the courters [people who lived in the courts] was to drink and fight'.

For working-class and poor families, the cramped housing simply was not enough to accommodate them all on an everyday basis, and it makes sense that family life and a neighbourly social life should spill out onto the streets. In 1893, a local newspaper, *The Liver*, noted that pavements were 'crowded with the fair sex standing in groups three to a dozen ... laughing hilariously as they relate "funny stories"'. This street society also gave women the opportunity to make emotionally deeper connections as they chatted around a doorstep, corner shop, or street barrow, offering friendship and support, and allowed their children to play freely without trashing their meagre homes while under the watchful eye of a streetful of 'Aunties'.

Despite the mid-century improvements, mortality in Liverpool was one of the highest in England, with a stark difference between inner city and suburb – two-and-a-half times higher in the slums than in the more open spaces further from the centre. Many families still lived in inadequate, cramped and unhealthy accommodation, such as the three-storey back-to-back houses which had been built by speculators on the former gardens of merchant's houses in Duke Street in the city centre. A true back-to-back shares a rear wall with another house of usually identical or very similar design, and these nine properties were still inhabited as late as the 1970s. Every part of the property was used, including, in the nineteenth century, the dark and damp cellars with their earth flooring, the back cellar room being the most unhealthy of all – as Dr Duncan wrote, it derived 'its scanty supply of light and air solely from the first apartment [cellar]'.

Liverpool Corporation made great efforts to provide better housing. Attractive terraced houses were built in the Bevington Street area and in Summer Seat (built in c.1911, see page 9) close to Scotland Road. These examples of 'corpy houses' were three bedroomed 'cottages' with an entrance and small vestibule, a living room, a scullery with sink, washboiler and bath, and a larder. Each house had its own hot-water supply heated by a boiler at the back of an open range in the living room. At the rear was an open yard, with an outside toilet and ashbin. Round the corner was Eldon Place, with its three blocks of corporation tenements constructed the following year. The development had 'garden city' touches such as mock Elizabethan details to the exterior, and open spaces with bandstand-like structures to sit in. Prior to this, more tenements had been built in Vauxhall in the 1890s. Victoria Square, as it was known, was regarded as model housing for artisans. The trend continued, and between 1919 and 1931, an impressive seventy per cent of all new property built in Liverpool was built by the corporation.

All in all, by 1900, there were many decent terraced properties in Liverpool, corporation or otherwise, with a front

AT HOME 9

Summer Seat, Vauxhall, c.1910. Two well dressed ladies walk down the partially completed street of social housing, designed to offer families safe and hygenic, if still basic, homes in which to enjoy life.

parlour, back kitchen or living room, scullery with tap, and three bedrooms. Simple decorative features such as cornices and ceiling roses added to the feeling of upward mobility, and a bay window in the parlour might house a large potted fern or aspidistra. A home of this size, which might be in a better area such as Everton, would cost 7s 6d per week in rent, and was for skilled workers rather than labourers. Sadly, not everyone appreciated the new housing, or the civic buildings erected in the Victorian era. John Rankin of Liverpool University, complained in 1907 of the 'miles of dull, monotonous and ugly streets in which not only the poor but the middle classes of the town are condemned to live' and declared that 'The building of the period has been … indescribably mean and ugly.' He also condemned the trend that had developed over the nineteenth century for different social classes to reside more and more in their own districts, which he noted were 'a physical barrier to the growth of this social spirit'. Presumably, as an academic at the university, and unlike many wives and mothers in Liverpool, he had the luxury of much more superior accommodation to choose from.

The Suburbs

Life in the pleasant suburbs in the early twentieth century was very different. A typical middle-class house for a professional family in, say, West Derby, Allerton, and Aigburth, might consist of lounge, dining room, sitting kitchen (where the maids sat, as one rarely if ever mixed with one's help), working kitchen, boiler house, outside WC for the maids and the gardener, two staircases (one for family and the other for staff), an indoor bathroom, and electricity and hot water throughout. A very large property might have its own tennis court or croquet lawn. In the early 1930s, a new home in Broadgreen would cost £900 and comprised three large bedrooms, two reception, kitchen bathroom, separate WC, garden, and modern facilities such as plentiful hot water. One's neighbours would be fellow professional or business people, and were the people with whom one would socialise. By 1939, sixty per cent of middle-class families were either in the process of buying their own homes, or already had bought one, part of a nationwide inter-war trend for speculative building and purchasing. As the twentieth century progressed, hundreds of semi-detached homes were built, some perhaps rather more compact than before, with a slightly smaller third bedroom but still with all conveniences. From c.1912, garden suburbs such as Hartley's Village in Aintree, and Wavertree Garden Suburb, further transformed the housing stock in which the city's women raised their children. In the late 1930s, the design for the Speke township was begun, with 72,000 new homes planned for Liverpool's families; a new industrial estate offered work to residents, as did large industrial complexes at Kirkby and Aintree. The council had a powerful input, using statutory powers to build twenty-nine factories. In a classic piece of social engineering, building began in 1939 on a large development encircled by green belt, suitable to house a social mix of families. After the 1939–45 war the plans were revised in 1947 to include a formal 'town centre' with two cinemas, parish church, open-air theatre and other amenities.

There were disadvantages to living in the new suburbs. The provision of facilities such as community centres and shopping parades could be slow to develop. Working-class women were accustomed to the support and camaraderie of the terraced streets and even slum housing. What was referred to by some as 'neighbouring' – that close contact between friends, and perhaps extended family in nearby streets, with ready support as and when you needed it, was difficult to replicate in the new suburbs. The aspirant residents of the better suburbs also had to adapt to a different lifestyle, and usually that meant less casual interaction with neighbours. Undoubtedly, some women rehoused into large corporation built estates such as Speke or Norris Green (built 1929 onwards) would have felt this isolation, and probably missed the female support networks even more than their middle-class 'sisters', while the stringent rules laid down by the council to their carefully chosen tenants may have felt restrictive, even draconian. Symptoms of low mood and anxiety were frequently reported, or at the least, boredom, until social and community opportunities evolved, and friendships made; the figures are probably higher than reported, as some families moved back to their original residential areas, unable to settle even in this brave new world of social housing.

Those born into the middle classes probably felt it equally, as newly married women were more likely to have had the stimulation of a career before marriage, and a 'daily' would do heavier and tedious chores – some families still had a live-in 'help' even in the 1930s, and there were plenty of Irish and Northern Welsh incomers keen to take the jobs – she might be a 'cook-general', with a washerwoman coming in to help on wash day. In upper-class houses, maids were always on hand to pick up the discarded clothes of the teenage daughters, and there was little incentive to learn how to run a home. Having paid help in the house meant fewer practical tasks for the housewife to do herself, and more time on her hands. The boredom, loss of work-based status and social life, sudden isolation, and lack of intellectual stimulation could cause depression and restlessness, especially if the first baby arrived within a year or so of the marriage. For middle-class women, it was almost as if the rigid 'separate spheres' of men and women, so much in favour in middle-class Victorian lives, had never really gone away. For the upper class women used to a life of leisure, they would continue with their golf and private dance parties, with the added status of being married and having a smart home.

Of course, not all women and girls were part of a family or household unit. Many itinerant women lived hand-to-mouth existences, begging, hawking or prostituting themselves. These women might sleep rough, or if they could, would find the money to pay night by night for a space in a lodging house. This might mean sharing a bed with another 'guest', or if you could afford it, having a bed to yourself. Anything up to 15,000 people a night sought space in a lodging house, or one of the better but still basic 'hotels', such as the Bevington Bush Hotel, aimed at artisans and respectable workers, paying 6*d* per night for the peace and quiet and cleanliness they offered, although in fact they were more like an early youth hostel in their semi-communal accommodation. Thousands of women were also in workhouses or infirmaries, or other forms of institution such as asylums and homes for fallen women.

Butties, Scouse and a Cuppa: feeding the family from the back kitchen

(*Butty: either a traditional sandwich with two slices of bread and filling; or in poorer houses, one slice of bread cut off a loaf and spread with jam, or sugar, condensed milk, chips etc, often folded over before eating*).

How well a woman could feed her family often depended on her income. In c.1910, a semi-skilled man was lucky to earn £1 per week, to keep himself, his wife and his children; his wife's skills as a frugal cook could be the difference between eating the day before payday, or not. Food was not thrown away if it was burnt; the pan and burnt food would simply be taken off the stove and sat in a few inches of cold water to release it, then served. If fresh cream was not available, a whipped-up egg white would be a good substitute. Stale bread was used in many ways, for puddings, toppings and so on, but it was never wasted. The skills of our foremothers in this period were passed on to their daughters and used to admirable effect during the Second World War.

'Tea' meant different things to different families. Working-class families might see this as the only meal of the evening, but for middle- and upper-class families it was a precursor to a later evening meal. Tea sets were a popular wedding present, and a display cabinet was the usual place to keep it; napkins and table cloths were also essential accessories for the 'ritual' of tea, and sitting down to tea and a snack was an important reinforcer of the family unit – the mother or significant female homemaker in a house prepared and served the tea, conversation and polite manners were practised, and visitors entertained. In the mid-nineteenth century this ritual was being taken out of the domestic sphere and into newly established tea shops, in the city and other gathering-places such as nearby seaside resorts on the Wirral and Fylde coast. Tea shops were an opportunity for women to meet together, unchaperoned, in an innocuous public setting – in this way, a private family ritual became a public one too.

In other homes, 'tea' might be a plate of Scouse. A modern 'gourmet' recipe for Scouse, with its chunky pieces of lamb, fresh herbs, a splash of artisan ale, and a rich stock, hardly resembles the cheap meal made by women all over Liverpool for their families. In practice, generations of families ate Scouse made with whatever root vegetables and meat were available, and often no meat in it at all ('blind scouse'). Any blandness may have been counteracted by a spoonful of pickle – red cabbage, beetroot – on the side of the plate.

'Inferior' food was an everyday occurrence for poor families – Engels mentions cocoa powder being adulterated with fine soil treated with fat to disguise it, tea leaves with added crushed sloe leaves or used tea leaves roasted to re-sell as fresh, and all manner of obnoxious substances added to tobacco to make it go further. Flour – an essential for baking day bread, pastry and if you were lucky, cakes – was padded out with gypsum or chalk. Alcohol was hardly of decent quality – port wine was manufactured directly from pure alcohol mixed with dyes, a popular drink with which one could shut out the grim drudgery of everyday life.

The *Sunlight Household Hints* booklet warned against adulterated sugar: 'The usual adulterants of sugar are sawdust and fine sand' and a way to test sugar's purity was to 'burn a little in an iron ladle … pure sugar will burn right away. Impure sugar will leave some ash behind it.' The booklet also warns of poisonous dyes found in some tinned fruits, and tinned meats that, if sealed incorrectly, caused the contents to go rancid.

For desperate families, charitable projects offered some relief. Liverpool's Christmas hot pot fund was described in glowing terms in an article in the *Harmsworth Magazine*. Six thousand poor families were provided with a large pan of stew – a 'hot pot' – which could be taken home and eaten as a family. The hot pots each contained 4lb of meat, 7lb of potatoes, and 1lb of

A group of girls waiting to collect a charitable hot pot for their families on Christmas Day, c.1900. Many charitable concerns in Liverpool relied solely upon public generosity to allow them to help the poor of the city.

onions, enough to feed a family of ten. The scheme operated via donations and each year needed about £1,200 to exist. Page 14 shows a group of young girls waiting to take hot pots home to their families – note their poor, ill-fitting clothes, gaunt faces, and some with cropped hair possibly due to head lice.

'Like priest and parsons, mothers have to live': Managing the budget

(Eleanor Rathbone, writing in the suffragette periodical *Common Cause*, 1912)

In 1909, Eleanor Rathbone (1872–1946), daughter of renowned local social reformer William Rathbone and herself a passionate social campaigner, despite a privileged upbringing, undertook a study published as *How the Casual Labourer Lives*. Rathbone and her team recruited numerous Liverpool families (often in the face of opposition from the husbands), and asked them to keep a record of what was earned, with every source of money recorded, what they spent, and what was bought, with an incentive of 4*d* (later raised to 6*d*) to keep going. It was clear from the study that the women did all the household budgeting, primarily using what their husband gave them if he was working, but many women did not know exactly how much their men earned, only what they expected from them weekly as 'housekeeping'.

Twenty-seven women kept their budget books for longer than four weeks, and of these, nineteen households had an income of less than 25*s* a week, with some going down to 15*s* or below if based on the husband's earnings alone. The families' budgets showed a 'feast and famine' approach to survival, spending relatively freely when the money was there and struggling during lean times; having a savings account to dip into was not an option on such low incomes. Loans and pawning helped a little, but the money still had to be found to make repayments and to redeem goods; only nine of the forty families Rathbone looked at were able to avoid these two options, and only two were completely debt-free. Household goods such as bedding and clothes – suits, bonnets, shirts and other linens – were cherished not because they were liked or offered pleasure aesthetically, but because the items had a value as pawnable goods; where a man was not working, his tool kit might also be pawned. Most women put goods into pawn on a Monday ready to pay the rent, and redeemed them on payday on Saturday, ready to buy food for the week and have the Sunday clothes ready for use. Families were keen to keep up payments on insurance policies, notably life insurance and burial funds, especially for their children, due to the high mortality rate.

Thanks to studies like this, Rathbone was increasingly convinced that the economic inequality of women was directly linked to their dependence as wives and mothers, and this informed her later campaigns. She believed that married women and mothers must have their own funds to draw on as a right – what later became known as Family Allowances, started out as a campaign for Family Endowments – Rathbone's Family Endowment Committee, produced a pamphlet, *Equal Pay and the Family: a proposal for the National Endowment of Motherhood.* Unfortunately, she also believed that working women accepted that they could never have parity with men's wages even for the same work, and a family allowance to 'reward' homemaking and motherhood duties would prevent women demanding equality in the workplace. Thus, if women had some money of their own, their husbands would make lower wage demands and the income of both genders would settle at a more equal level. She stepped up her campaign at the end of the First World War, and it was at this point that she encountered determined opposition from the NUWSS (National Union of Women's Suffrage Societies) leader, Millicent Fawcett, who took the Victorian view that such benefits made people lazy about looking after their own children. Still other feminists felt Eleanor's idea was repressive, tying women to their homes and husbands in order to receive the small payout, while trade unionists worried about the destabilising effect the scheme may have on wages.

In 1924, Rathbone wrote the influential *The Disinherited Family* which put forward the economic case for reform of family incomes that economist and reformer (and author of the

1942 Beveridge Report) William Beveridge declared converted him to the principle of family allowances. In 1934, Eleanor formed the Children's Minimum Committee, which aimed to ensure that no child should be denied a minimum standard of living because of their parent's poverty. Eleanor continued to campaign vigorously for family allowances into the 1940s.

Clothing the family

Keeping a family – and oneself – decently clothed was a challenge. Garments had a higher overall value than second-hand clothes today, and often served as many as five owners before being discarded, subjected to many alterations or passed round the family till unwearable. All girls learned to darn, patch and mend as part of their education, both at home and school; for example, turning collars (taking off the collar and sewing it back with the un-frayed side on the upper side), or unravelling woollen garments and re-knitting them. If they were not buying from second-hand shops or rag markets, poor families also fell prey to the trickery of purveyors of cheap cloth and clothing – for example, stretching fabrics such as flannel as far as it could go so that on the first wash, it would shrink badly and no longer fit the person it was bought for.

Whatever clothes you could afford, it was an onerous task to look after them, even in the 1930s. Hand washing, using tubs, copper boilers, the sink and a variety of wash boards was still the norm for most families. Trimming was removed from garments prior to washing, as the unstable dyes in them could run into it. Many fabrics shrank badly – one woman told the author about her experience of buying a crepe de chine frock in a multi-coloured design, from Lewis's, the department store:

> I had to wash it by hand, and ooh! The dye that came out of it! And when you had got it wet, it shrunk up to nothing. You had to carefully iron it back to its 'dry' size before you could wear it again, but I had to sew the lace collar back on it as well before I could put it on.

Shoes were lined with paper or cardboard because there was no money for repairs. Particularly in the nineteenth century, both children and their mothers living in terrible poverty could often be seen with no footwear at all. Decent boots, shoes and clogs needed to be carefully looked after – they were an expensive item and would be passed to a younger sibling if a child outgrew them. Waterproofing shoes was difficult – one remedy was to stand boots in linseed oil with some added castor oil for about three days, so they were completely saturated. (*Sunlight Household Hints*). If footwear was not well oiled and supple, it quickly dried out and the leather, might crack or shrink – rescue remedies included linseed oil, egg yolks, gum Arabic, ink, and kerosene, and having all these ingredients ready for any domestic necessity – and using them – would have been expensive and time consuming. Moths were a perennial problem, and popular deterrents were camphor, and cedar wood. Looking after a family at this time was a challenge, often made worse by restricted wages and poor housing, and every woman had to cope with her individual challenges in her own way.

CHAPTER TWO

Health and Welfare

Family Health

Prior to the National Health Service, the majority of poor families would have to look after themselves as best they could, with charitable institutions, or the workhouse infirmary as a last resort. Female neighbours helped out, and there was always one who was more knowledgeable than the rest who could suggest home remedies. Again, the *Sunlight Household Hints* booklet gives insights into the 'self-help' home-nursing methods of the times, suggesting butter as an ointment for 'all sorts of bruises, cuts, chaps, or roughness of the skin'. The majority of families in the mid-nineteenth century would be solely reliant on over the counter remedies, family advice and support (particularly from female friends, neighbours and relatives), and common sense. Chest and intestinal problems, and epidemics such as diptheria, whooping cough, and influenza were particularly frightening – the mortality rate from chest disease was sixty per cent higher than the national average and that from epidemics was one-and-a-half times the national average. Even before the discovery of the 'germ theory' in the 1860s, good ventilation and disinfecting were accepted as vital tools in the fight against illness, and even later in the nineteenth century, the *Sunlight Household Hints* booklet was keen to remind housewives of their duties in this regard.

Motherhood

A first-time mother would often go into her marriage with a baby's layette already prepared in her 'bottom drawer', a term used for the items a young woman had carefully prepared for her future life as wife and mother. Night dresses, day dresses, shawls, binders, nappies, bonnets and bibs were all carefully stored. These items would be used over and over again for each baby, but of course not all babies lived, and some mothers bought an extra yard or two of flannel cloth, big enough to completely wrap the baby in, just in case she or he did not survive. If the baby thrived and grew bigger, the cloth could always be used to make undergarments for the child – or kept for the next time.

When it was time for the mother's 'lying in', middle-class women did have access to the services of a doctor or live-in midwife, and latterly to pain relief such as chloroform; but those who had looked after themselves and rested as they felt the need, were blamed if they had a tough labour for their habit of 'soft' living. Working-class women, such as the ones in the appalling slums of Liverpool, apparently had no bother at all giving birth – or perhaps it was more the case that it was pointless to complain. Doctors asked: if a servant girl could excuse herself from work for a couple of hours, go and give birth, and then present herself for work again, what was wrong with affluent women? Yet at the same time, domestic servants who did this were also condemned as immoral and uncaring. With the high mortality rates at the time, surely all women feared childbirth, or injury to their child and themselves.

There was a growing conviction in the medical profession that there must be more hospital provision for pregnant women and their babies, at all stages of gestation, the birth, and afterwards. Inadequate home conditions – anything from lack of privacy to unclean environments, incompetent female midwives, multiple births, and numerous other birth-related dangers, were all reasons put forward for closer monitoring of mothers and babies, and the increased likelihood of medical intervention – a male 'medicalisation' of childbirth. As early as 1796, the Ladies

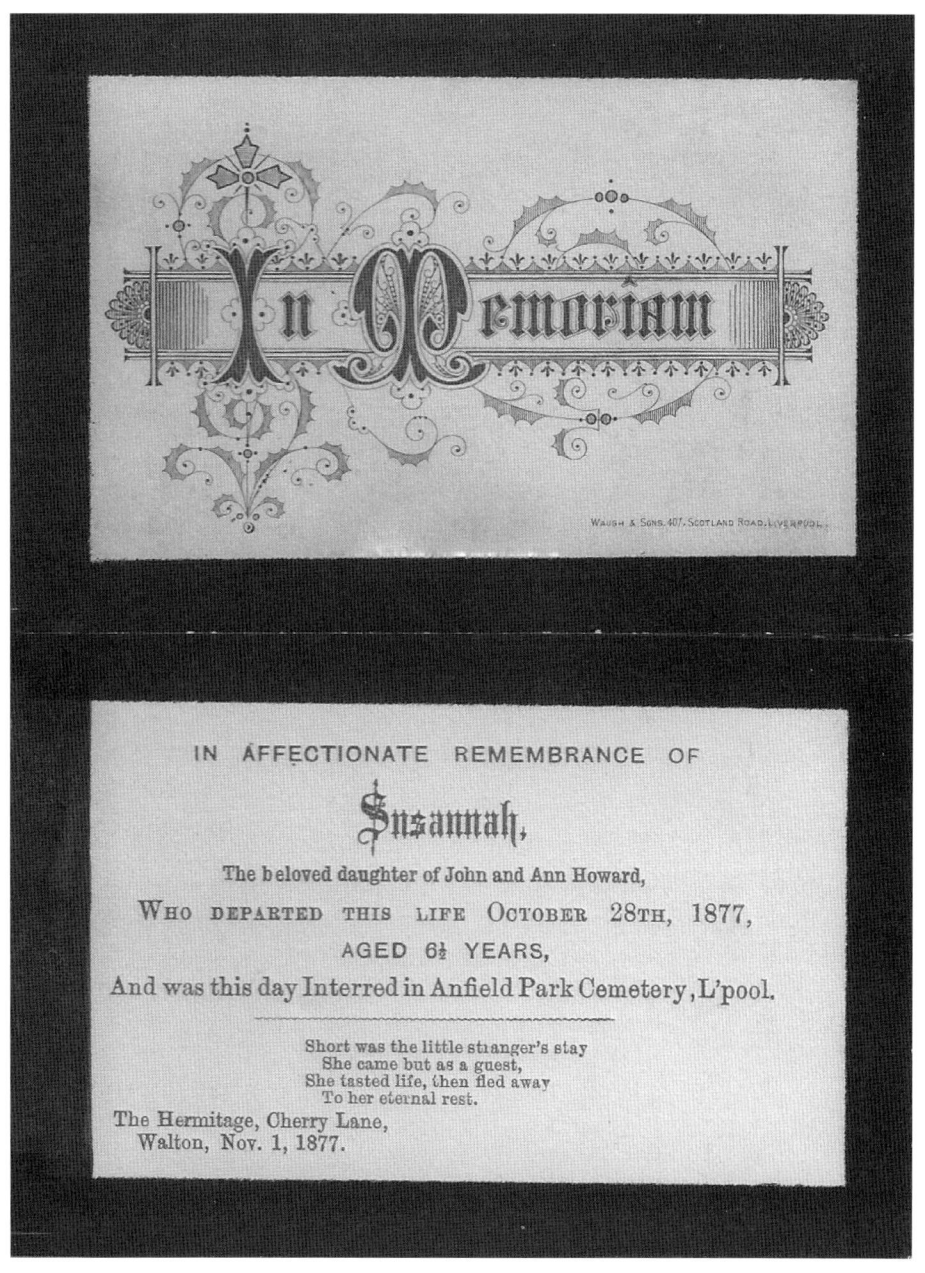

Women of all classes in the nineteenth and early twentieth centuries had to cope with high levels of infant and child mortality, exacerbated by the prevalence of epidemics of childhood diseases such as measles and diptheria.

Charity was established at 13 School Lane, and in 1869, the charity amalgamated into the separate Lying-In Hospital and Dispensary for the Diseases of Women and Children which was established in 1841, and located at 31 Horatio Street, Scotland Road, relocating to larger premises at 21 Pembroke Place in October 1845. This was no place for a fallen woman to get help, however – unmarried mothers were not admitted. This last rule lost the charity a £50 donation, because the donor disapproved of such a draconian decision. In 1883, the hospital for the general care of women moved to Shaw Street, and in 1932 it amalgamated with the Samaritan Hospital for Women (first opened in 1895). A maternity hospital was built in Oxford Street 1924–26.

'No amateur work': Nursing Services, Hospitals and the Nursing Profession

('No amateur work': Florence Nightingale's opinion of the role of nursing, in her introduction to *The Organisation of Nursing in a Large Town*, a book about the Liverpool nurses' training centre and home.)

In 1858, Florence Nightingale visited Liverpool, and gave two lectures to the National Association for the Promotion of Social Science. She offered an expert critique of hospital design, construction, management, and practice. Her vision was to have hospitals in which all these factors came together harmoniously, and even if patients could not be cured, the hospital should do no harm to anyone. The state of hospital provision in Liverpool at that time was questionable. The original Liverpool Royal Infirmary was built in 1824 on Brownlow Hill, and was quickly outgrown by the rising population, failing to provide the medical services and educational facilities that the city needed. Nightingale's lectures encouraged a genuine desire to rebuild the city's hospital services. Such refurbishments take time, however, and it was not until November 1889 that the new infirmary opened. The design was mindful of all the points raised by Nightingale and others. It included fire-resisting features, four circular wards (which used space economically), eight pavilion 'Nightingale wards', a large chapel, an operating theatre with a viewing gallery for 200 people, outpatients facilities, and ample ventilation throughout. It was hoped that the 290 beds would serve the city well for decades to come. The hospital was managed by a board of trustees who had the onerous task of fundraising, in the days before the National Health Service, which took over management in 1948. By 1887, nurses trained at the Nightingale school were working not only at the Royal Infirmary, but also the Workhouse Infirmary and the Southern Infirmary (see page 25, photograph of the Jenny Lind ward). In addition, a training school and nurses' home, organised by William Rathbone, opened in 1862 in Ashton Street under the stewardship of Miss Mary Merryweather as superintendent, and her sister Elizabeth as deputy, until 1874. Mary was born in 1818 in Dorset to a Quaker family, had spent many years as a 'moral missionary' and was trained in nursing in London before moving to Liverpool – her professional, moral and religious credentials as a safe pair of hands at the training school were impeccable. She faced considerable challenges when recruiting, having to dismiss trainees for being 'dirty and dishonest' (Annie Rogerson), 'parted with for insobriety' (Mary Mathews), or even 'totally unfit'.

Liverpool Royal Infirmary, c.1900. Designed by Alfred Waterhouse, the building was architecturally striking and an ultra-modern hospital for the times. The first patients were admitted in 1889.

Nevertheless, many women were successfully trained in Liverpool and went on to work to an excellent standard in voluntary hospitals, district nursing, and also the private nursing of wealthy patients and affluent mothers during their lying-in. The new building offered accommodation on three floors, with the nurses sleeping in dormitories, while matron had her own sitting room and bedroom; downstairs, there was a dining room and a visitor's room. There were two types of trainee – the lady pupil, who paid for her year's full-time training, and the probationer, a woman of more limited means who was paid a very small wage for working and training at the same time, over four years – in 1871, the vast majority of the trainee nurses in Miss Merryweather's care were described as probationers, and they came from all parts of the nation. The trainees from middle-class families, who had received a grammar-school education, generally worked at the Royal Infirmary – sadly, sectarianism seemed to infiltrate even the nursing profession, as the Royal Infirmary was happy to take Welsh nurses, but much more reluctant to recruit from the Irish community; it also favoured entrants from the southern counties. Voluntary hospitals such as the David Lewis Northern regularly recruited local girls. The Poor Law hospitals, as in Smithdown Road and Walton, did take Irish girls, and because such hospitals sometimes struggled to recruit enough nurses, entrance requirements were 'flexible' in order to maintain numbers on the wards. Whatever their background, unmarried status was essential. Nursing was an appealing occupation for many women, as it offered accommodation, food, a wage, and a significantly higher status than domestic service by this time. The training was practical, with placements on different wards – medical, surgical, and so on – to give the probationers and newly qualified nurses every chance to learn on the job. The nurses shared the night shifts. Probationers were expected to make and apply dressings, cook for patients, attend operations, manage the movement of patients, maintain the highest standards of cleanliness, and adhere to many other stringent rules and codes of conduct as set out in the rules of the training school. Such was the influence of Florence Nightingale on the development

HEALTH AND WELFARE 25

The Jenny Lind ward, Royal Southern Hospital. Note the predominance of female nurses and staff in the ward. Nursing was seen as a suitable career for women as it was seen to complement a woman's innate capacity for nurturing.

of nursing in Liverpool, that she was honoured in a stained-glass window, in which the image of the pioneering nurse was accompanied by a Rathbone District Nurse, and a ward sister.

Sometimes it was not practical to admit women to a hospital, or even necessary, even if they did need medical attention – for them, community nursing was the answer. William Rathbone was a true philanthropist, with a genuine desire to understand the causes of poverty in Liverpool, and do all he could to alleviate it. When his wife became chronically sick, he employed a private nurse, Mary Robinson, to look after her. His wife died in 1859, and Rathbone resolved to make such personalised nursing services available to all, not just those with disposable income. The obvious person to seek advice from was Florence Nightingale, who strongly felt that nursing should not end at the hospital gate, but extend naturally into the community. In 1859, Rathbone established the District Nursing Service. A district nurse was so named because she was attached to one of four districts in the city – north, east, west, and central. Florence Nightingale had suggested that nurses be trained at the Royal Infirmary, with a proportion diverted off to form the community nursing section.

The service grew rapidly, and by 1867 there were eighteen districts in all, staffed by properly trained nurses bringing basic care to the sick and the poor, in their own homes; each district nurse cost £30–£40 per year to provide. In 1897, monies raised during the commemorations of Queen Victoria's reign, plus a donation from the David Lewis Trust, was all put to good use to expand the district nursing service, and this resulted in the formation of the Liverpool Queen Victoria District Nursing Association and the opening of the Central Home for District Nurses at 1, Princes Street. District nursing was very different to today's service – the nurse provided beds, nightwear, bedding, simple remedies, and medical equipment on loan to poor families recommended to the service, and her role as much as anything was to teach poor families how to look after their sick relatives themselves. Priority was initially given to tuberculosis patients in the final stages of their illness, and those who, for whatever reason, could not be accommodated in hospital. One new district nurse was so distressed by the scenes of abject poverty she witnessed, that after a week she declared that she could not carry on in the role and that she wanted to return to her previous job of home nursing the affluent; she did persist, however, and was soon thrilled by the difference she could make to the disadvantaged families she visited. There was an element of social work – wives who had fallen gravely ill, and their homes and families had fallen into chaos, with the husbands drinking heavily because they could not cope with their inability to help their wife – the district nurse showed the husbands how to home-nurse their wives, and the households settled down once more. On another occasion, the nurse washed and fed the child of a sick woman and saw her off to school. Other patients had more familiar problems – asthma, long-term cancer patients, infections and abscesses. On rare occasions, patients were removed from a nurse's books if they consistently refused to put into practice her advice. Other charitable organisations worked in tandem with the district nursing service, providing packages of invalid foods and supplies to families, and charities such as the Central Relief Society provided meat for some patients and convalescence at the seaside. Local churches were closely involved, although this was a purely secular organisation. As the Home and Training School noted in its report, the district nurse was an 'educated, refined and virtuous woman' whose work offers her 'peace and enlargement of soul'.

Public Health Initiatives

Infant mortality rates in nineteenth-century Liverpool were three times higher than in other parts of the country: 150.3 per 1,000 in the first month of life, to an astonishing 492 per 1,000 between 9 and 12 months. In general terms, ports such as Liverpool provided some of the unhealthiest living conditions in the nation compared to inland industrialised cities. In the Victorian era, opinions on public health were coloured by what now seems to be mere superstition – it was thought that overcrowding and insanitary conditions led to a damaging 'physical miasma', that is, the belief that infectious diseases emanated from bad air from rotting animal and vegetable matter (it was not until the 1860s that Louis Pasteur, in France, identified and developed the 'germ theory' of disease). Dr William Duncan believed firmly in these 'bad effluvias' and was determined to see improvements in ventilation and overall construction of buildings for Liverpool's poor families. By 1850, Liverpool had its own public wash-house – the world's first – in Upper Frederick Street. Rather like a chapel in appearance, the building was a revolution in cleanliness, with bath and washing facilities, a washroom for infected clothes, reading room, waiting room, and parlour. Women each had a cubicle to themselves to work on their laundry, with low partitions so they could chat together as they worked if they wanted to – the social aspect of visiting a wash-house was, for some, as important as the practical purpose. For those who had access to it, the wash-house must have been a revelation in its décor and facilities, but only to those who could afford the entrance fee, and many a woman continued to struggle with the insanitary conditions that made raising a large family so challenging. Catherine 'Kitty' Wilkinson (1786–1860) and her husband Thomas, who had come over from Ireland in 1812, were the first superintendents of the wash-house. Kitty had always been passionate about cleanliness, having previously invited her neighbours to use her kitchen to wash clothes during the 1832 cholera epidemic; however, she also looked to a widening of education as a way of encouraging understanding of hygiene, self-respect, and seeking better prospects in life – perhaps the reading room at the washhouse reflected her commitment to giving reading lessons to her neighbours. Although Kitty retired in 1853, her legacy continued, and a portrait of her was displayed in every washhouse erected in Liverpool, and she was commemorated in a stained glass window in the Lady Chapel of the Anglican Cathedral.

Campaigns to improve public health continued throughout the nineteenth century. In 1863, Liverpool began the switch from night closets (also known as soil closets) to water closets, which of course did not need emptying by the 'night soil man'. In 1857, a continuous supply of clean water was brought to the city for the first time with the creation of reservoirs near Bolton, and in 1880 the creation of Lake Vyrnwy in Wales increased the water supply for the growing population. Gradually, conditions in the city's homes were improving.

Institutions

As with every other community, there were women in Liverpool who, for whatever reason, could not look after themselves – the reasons might be financial, physical illness, old age, pregnancy, moral condemnation ('fallen women'), addiction, abandonment, deliberate distancing from family and support networks, mental health problems, or disability of all kinds. From the point of view of those managing the city's poor relief, the obvious place to place such vulnerable women was the workhouse.

The Liverpool workhouse originally stood on the site now occupied by the Metropolitan Cathedral, but had its early origins in 1770 with the establishment of the Liverpool Poor House. It was reconstructed on this site in 1824, to accommodate 1,800 inmates, but the demand soon outgrew its facilities, and in an attempt to keep up with that demand, the workhouse evolved into a rambling complex of buildings, the biggest workhouse in England, with at least 4,000 inmates at the beginning of the twentieth century. All the workhouses had similar conditions.

In the early 1850s, Nathaniel Hawthorne was invited to visit the workhouse at West Derby, and he wrote down his impressions of the place and the people:

> We were shown into a room where paupers are received on their first arrival; and the superintendent of this room was a bright, cheerful woman, between eighty and ninety years old. She has been a good many years in the workhouse, and has learnt to knit since she was seventy; and kept her fingers busily employed all the time she was talking to us…
>
> In the next room, was the domicile of an old man and his wife; for the authorities sometimes allow old married people to live together, when there is no risk of their increasing the population of the Work-House. In another room, there was an old lady, alone, and reading; a respectable looking, intelligent old soul, with rather more refined manners than the others; so I took my hat off in her room. There was a row of books on the mantlepiece, mostly religious but with a romance among them…
>
> …everywhere there were comfortable coal-fires in the open fire-places, and the women sitting quietly about them, all knitting as fast as their fingers would go. They looked well-fed and decently clothed in blue-checked gowns, all of one fashion; but none of them had a brisk cheerful air, except two or three very old persons, to

> whom a childish vivacity seemed to have returned with their extreme age. ...
>
> ...(there) was an old lady who declared herself to be more than a hundred years old ... the cheerfulest and jauntiest person in the house ... and so she seems to make herself a kind of old pet, whom people talk to as if she were a child, and she gives wayward, childish, half-playful answers.

This glowing account is at odds with the scenes observed by Josephine Butler, who in the oakum room found 200 inmates working while they sat on a cold, damp floor. Violence was common in the workhouse, with attacks on staff and fellow inmates; one matron was beaten to death by a dozen violent female inmates. Josephine was so moved by the squalor that she established a rest home for incurables, followed by an industrial school for destitute girls, to give them a training in skills such as laundry work and envelope making. Such was her empathy with her downtrodden 'sisters' that she even cared lovingly for some in her own home.

When it came to nursing care for these vulnerable women and other inmates, the initial situation was precarious in the infirmary. Unqualified older women, often not always in the best of health themselves and frequently drunk, were the so-called nursing staff; some were prostitutes. Poor standards of hygiene were common, a very dangerous practice in an institution with so many people living at close quarters – beds were changed once a month, and patients stayed in the same nightshirt for seven weeks at a time. The food was sub-standard for an invalid diet, in quality and content. Alcohol was freely smuggled onto the wards. Eleanor Rathbone, in her memoir of her father, William, wrote that these untrained and inadequate nurses were supervised by a few untrained parish officers, who felt the need to wear kid gloves when on the workhouse wards, to prevent their hands being contaminated. There were even police patrols in the infirmary, to keep order at night. William Rathbone turned to his trusted 'mentor', Florence Nightingale, for advice. She recommended the appointment of a nurse of the highest standards of training,

AGNES JONES, THE HOSPITAL NURSE.

Agnes Jones (1832–1868), the first fully trained nursing superintendent of Liverpool Workhouse Infirmary. Already weakened by overwork as she strove to improve conditions for her patients, Agnes died of typhus fever in 1868.

practice, and character to reform the infirmary, and suggested Miss Agnes Jones, a devout and gifted nurse, who accepted the appointment in August 1864 and arrived at the workhouse with a team of twelve qualified nurses in 1865.

Agnes Jones was a favourite of Florence's, because she had the level of training and family background Florence required in a nurse. In short, Agnes was someone trusted to make a difference to what Nightingale found on a visit to Liverpool to be a situation 'far more untameable than any lion'. Rathbone paid for Miss Jones to take up this role, and she was to be the pioneer of the training in a workhouse infirmary. Pioneers challenge existing practices and mindsets, and Agnes faced resistance from the administrators of the workhouse due to her very high standards and strict discipline. She had a difficult working relationship with the governor of the workhouse, who described her as 'a stiff-necked Presbyterian Irishwoman from Ulster with a hot Irish temper.' More than once, Florence had to act as peacemaker in the disputes. However, in time, the high standards imposed on the infirmary began to have a positive impact. With trained nurses delivering outstanding care and patients receiving decent quality, nutritious food, Agnes finally transformed conditions in the infirmary – at less cost to the administrators, but great personal cost to herself. In the winter of 1867, Agnes had 1,350 patients to care for with her team, and she was lucky to get four hours sleep a night. In 1868, physically and mentally exhausted, she succumbed to typhus and died on 19 February. Florence Nightingale, while saddened by the death of such a fine woman, was also concerned that the standards she had striven for would now decline, so she wrote to the infirmary nurses and urged them to continue with their excellent work.

Women with mental health challenges might be placed in one of several places. The workhouse was a useful starting point, as a person too mentally ill to work could be labelled as a pauper lunatic and placed there – so long as she remained relatively docile. If she exhibited challenging behaviour, she could be moved to the local lunatic asylum. Liverpool had had some provision for the mentally ill since the late eighteenth century, in the form of the Liverpool Lunatic Asylum, but it was unable to cope with the demands placed on it, and following the County Asylums and Lunacy Acts of 1845, the third Lancashire County Asylum was built in Rainhill. It opened on 1 January 1851, and was the primary destination for Liverpudlian paupers with mental health illnesses. Improvements and extensions continued over the years in response to overcrowding and the pressures on the service, and by 1936 it had 3,000 patients, the biggest such facility in the country.

The 1881 census gives an insight into the female population of the asylum at that time. Of the 359 female inmates, the majority were women in their thirties and forties, with women in their fifties a close second. There were however a sizable number in their twenties – fifty of them – but relatively low numbers in the sixty-plus age bracket, suggesting that those suffering from dementia remained in the workhouse where possible. At least half of the women were born in Liverpool or other towns in Lancashire, mainly the larger ones, and 118 were born in Ireland. Marital status was split fairly evenly between married and unmarried, with a surprisingly low number (forty-four) declared as widows. This being the asylum for the poor, few of their stated occupations are beyond the low paid or any pay at all, with 147 housewives, 114 in domestic service, and a scattering of other occupations including governess, school teacher, fustian cutter, hawker, lace dyer, and actress. It is interesting to note that the isolation and extreme fatigue felt by lone domestic servants – the 'maid of all work' – was known to lead to depression and even breakdowns, and the challenges faced by poor married women struggling to raise a family and make ends meet must have led to similar problems. Of the staff who cared for them under the management of clinician Thomas Lawes Rogers, there are more than enough females to care for the women inmates, all unmarried or widows, and born in places across the country – only a relatively small number were local. Poignantly, tucked away in the lists of the asylum staff, is a 2-week-old baby boy, 'child of an inmate'. His place of birth is given as the asylum itself.

Women did not always spend their lives in an asylum once admitted. With rest, decent food and the rudimentary talking therapies on offer, some could, and did, recover from acute episodes and were released. The many stories that abound concerning 'immoral' or fallen women and girls being incarcerated in asylums following some perceived misbehaviour often have a foundation in truth, but it would be unfair to condemn all of these institutions out of hand. If nothing else, they provided a refuge for the distressed and respite from fraught family situations.

Illegitimacy, and provision for 'Fallen Women'

Even though marriage was considered a prerequisite to children, equally there were a substantial number of women who gave birth to illegitimate children. Such women were referred to as having 'fallen' – morally, from favour, from grace, and from the respectable echelons of society. It was a source of much anguish among social commentators and activists, and the issue of what was to be done with such flawed females was a hot topic for decades.

By the end of the nineteenth century, there was a bewildering array of institutions, that could take in a woman in distress, often a woman who had 'fallen' and was pregnant with, or had already given birth to, an illegitimate child. The Gore's Directory of Liverpool and Birkenhead for 1900 lists a number of institutions for fallen women, such as the Ellen Cliff Home for Fallen Women and The Home (for fallen women). Many children's homes would not take illegitimate children, the result of their mother's 'fall', and the only one in the directory which clearly states it will take children born out of wedlock is the Medina Home for Children:

> This institution receives illegitimate, destitute and orphan children, and assists young girls who have made the first slip from virtue to obtain situations and thus have an opportunity to retrieve their character and once more to return to the path of virtue and respectability.

Another institution which took in 'fallen women' and their babies was the House of Providence Home for Desolate Women, also in Liverpool. It was opened in 1891 by Monsignor James Nugent, 'The Father of the Poor', a well-known and much-loved social campaigner, and it was a haven for fallen women who had just had their first – and hopefully only – illegitimate baby.

The Monsignor was another activist who thought 'first timers' had a better chance of being redeemed than habitual offenders. In an impassioned letter to the *Liverpool Mercury*, in December 1900, Monsignor Nugent said,

> Amid the joyous surroundings of the great festival [Christmas] there comes the wail of many heart-broken and destitute fellow creatures ... none more utterly desolate than the poor unfortunate female, who, through circumstances of misplaced confidence or otherwise, has become a mother, and finds herself basely deceived and cruelly deserted, with a helpless infant to provide for. So many ... seek to end their trouble by resorting to child murder and suicide. Spurned by their partners in guilt, and ostracised by their own kith and kin.... Help me to save them from despair and ruin! They can be rescued if we but stretch forth a helping hand.

Monsignor Nugent goes on to describe his home:

> The House of Providence, at West Dingle, Liverpool, affords a safe refuge for these neglected and forlorn ones, and at present over 40 unwedded mothers, with their helpless babes, find that shelter and protection ... denied them by outraged friends and society ... poor ruined girls, left alone in the World, penniless, without home or friends, out on the streets, starving in the midst of plenty.

Finally this tireless campaigner makes his appeal for donations:

> help me to rescue them from the perils to which they are exposed ... the cry of these forsaken and deserted creatures, mingling with the mute entreaty of their hapless babes, must surely reach every Christian and compassionate heart ... spare at least a little to help forward this great work for the rescue of the fallen. Any contributions of old clothing, &co, or materials from which garments can be made, would be very acceptable.

The *Tablet* journal of November 1899 also described the building's 'lofty and capacious dormitory' and 'well appointed nursery.' The home supported over 200 women and their babies between 1897 and 1905.

When the campaigning priest died in 1907, a statue was erected in his honour, which among other accolades, described the Monsignor as a 'Saviour of Fallen Womanhood'.

Despite the best efforts of the moral and social workers, illegitimacy continued, and at times, there was an increase in numbers due to national circumstances. During both world wars, an atmosphere of 'seize the day' led to a loosening of moral strictures, and more single, widowed, or even married, women embarked on affairs that ended in an illegitimate baby, or one for whom her husband was not the biological father. During the First World War, the birth rate for babies born outside marriage rose from 4.29% in 1913, to 6.26% in 1918, which looks a small increase, but in statistical and cultural terms was significant. This was despite the efforts of the Liverpool Women's Police Patrol, which was established in 1914 because of increased worries about immorality in the city. The founders, Lydia Booth and Edith Wright, initially saw their role to be the 'policing' of women's morality for the duration of the war, with thousands of servicemen passing through the port bringing the potential for increased sexual immorality. By the end of the Second World War, the illegitimacy rate had risen to nine per cent; there were 63,420 illegitimate births registered in 1945, compared to 25,633 in 1939. During the war, the government issued a leaflet reminding women – 'girls' in particular (that is, young single women), to guard not only against this atmosphere of laissez-faire, but also against unwittingly leading men on and getting into a 'no turning back' situation:

> Many women easily arouse in men the desire for physical contacts and the expression of sex.... If this power is deliberately used by a girl who has no intention of giving way ... [she] will soon gain a most unenviable reputation [and] a man whose desires have been excited may be driven to that type of woman who merely gratifies the

man's physical sex hunger.... Such women give him neither friendship nor help, but all too often they do give him venereal disease ... [Another girl] may find to her dismay that without realizing what she was doing she has gone further than she ever intended.

(*Women in Wartime* leaflet, issued by the Central Council for Health Education, c.1939).

The main point of the leaflet was to prevent sexual encounters in order to keep rates of sexually transmitted infections low, which would have safeguarded public health, and also prevented unwanted babies whilst maintaining a level of moral decorum. For many women and girls, the advice clearly went unheeded. The advice also seemed to absolve men from any reponsiblity, and suggests that if men do get beyond the point of self-control, the female partner alone is to blame for her careless encouragement. Conditioned as they were to shoulder the blame for unwanted sexual encounters, some female victims of sexual assaults must have been discouraged from reporting the attack to the police.

Other help for mothers and their children

In the early 1900s, Eleanor Rathbone became involved in the Victoria Women's Settlement, which was managed by Elizabeth Macadam, a Scottish social worker who also greatly improved the training for social workers at the university; in 1913, Rathbone brought out the *Report on the Liverpool Women's Industrial Council Survey of Widows Under the Poor Law.* Her social activism, informed by her in-depth knowledge of the social problems of the poor, led to her view that widows should have a pension separate to the poor relief:

The widow who is doing her duty by her young children, tending them, washing, sewing and cooking for them, is not a pensioner upon the bounty of the state, but is earning the money she draws from it by services just as valuable to the community as those of a dock-labourer, a plumber, or a soldier.

To many of Eleanor's contemporaries, this was an unconventional proposal, but her growing conviction that all women who were mothers and homemakers should have the dignity of what was essentially a wage for their work, was nothing short of revolutionary for the times. She found it unacceptable that mothers were so economically dependent on others (usually their husband and/or the father of their children). However, it was not until the advent of the welfare state that proper financial support was introduced for women in different circumstances.

CHAPTER THREE

Toil and Trouble: Women at Work

◆

Anyone with a 'traditionalist' view of history may assume that our foremothers had little impact on the world of work, and that they were primarily homemakers and wives. This is undoubtedly true for some women, but patently untrue for others, while more still had a mixed relationship with work depending on their age and marital, social and economic status.

A group of staff outside the Central Café, c.1928–30. Table waitresses, 'front of house', kitchen staff and others are all represented here. Café and restaurant work was tiring but, in a respectable establishment, offered more independence and status than domestic service in a private home.

The census is an invaluable source for a survey of women's work, but as any family historian knows, it is not without its challenges. Some enumerators, although under instruction to record faithfully all information given, could not see the value of putting down a woman's occupation, and one can find impoverished enumeration districts where apparently all the women lived a life of leisure. In other examples, it is possible that the attitudes within a certain household or family influenced their answers. In 1851, at No 3 Court, Maddock Street (in the area of Scotland Road), 28-year-old Ellien Clark is listed with her husband Thomas, a coachman. Her occupation is stated dismissively as 'wife'. While today the role of 'Home Maker' is often used in census returns and elsewhere, this enumerator uses this descriptor only in Ellien's census entry, so it is possible that that is what was stated by either Thomas, or both of them. Other women, married to tradesmen of all kinds, were described on the census as, for example, 'grocer's wife', when her role in the family business may have been crucial to its success.

Domestic Service

> **WANTED**, in a gentleman's family, a thorough general SERVANT. Must be a good plain cook and well recommended. Good wages. – Apply at 43, Bold Street.
>
> (*Liverpool Mercury*, 4 February 1870)

In the mid-Victorian era, when opportunities for women's work in Liverpool were limited, domestic service work was always available, and in the upmarket area around Abercromby Square in the census for that year, some of the rich merchants' houses had up to a dozen servants. Here, living comfortably on her own means in what has been referred to as 'Liverpool's Bloomsbury', was Mrs Christian Paton, a widow with her two unmarried daughters, Marion and Ann, both in their thirties; three grandchildren who are at school, and grandson, William, a share broker. All but granddaughter Charlotte were born in Scotland – Charlotte, whose surname is Jones, was born in Liverpool. To look after

TOIL AND TROUBLE: WOMEN AT WORK 41

An unnamed woman in maid's uniform, c. 1915–20, photographed by De Freyne, 1A Lorton Street. This woman wears a typical outfit for a restaurant, hotel, or upper class household of the day. In some establishments, the cost of her uniform would be deducted from her wages.

this relatively large family are three servants: a male butler, and two females. The housemaid, Janet Jones, is 27 years old, born in Wrexham in N.E. Wales, and the 19-year-old cook, Jane Lewis, was born in Dyserth in Flintshire (N.E. Wales). It was not unusual for domestic servants to travel from North Wales to work in affluent households in Liverpool, and send money back to their families, often not seeing their own homes and relatives for many months at a time. A few came from further afield, even Ceredigion and down into Merionthshire, although the majority were concentrated closer to Liverpool. Domestic servants also came from along the Lancashire and Cumbrian coastline, the Midlands, Cheshire, and inland Lancashire.

Employers often made specific demands in their advertisements. A survey of nineteenth-century advertisements in Liverpool newspapers reveals that a significant percentage of employers stipulated 'Protestants only', and there was even an employment agency in Liverpool that catered to this very requirement:

> **PRINCE'S PARK PROTESTANT REGISTRY**, No 4, Carter Street, Prince's Road. – Waitresses, Cooks, Housemaids, Nurses, and first class Servants of every description Wanted. – Mrs Lofgren, proprietress.
>
> (*Liverpool Mercury*, 4 February 1870)

Other advertisements are brutally specific: 'Protestant, not Irish'; 'Must be a member of the Church of England'. There is clear discrimination here against Irish and/or Roman Catholic women; the forthright comments of the likes of Engels and others, along with ingrained prejudices and adoption of misinformation as fact, undoubtedly coloured the opinions of the non-Irish, Protestant population of the city. This was a division that, on occasion, flared into open hostility.

For the single 'maid of all work', who in the mid-nineteenth century earned between 9d to 1s per week plus bed and food, isolation from family and friends was a common complaint, and the servants could not, of course, befriend female members of the employing family or have a man friend. Where service in a private household did not appeal, the many hotels and lodging houses offered plenty of work – the London and North Western Hotel on Lime Street had 180 bedrooms with a highly transient guest population of railway travellers and many Americans who had recently arrived from New York; this would offer ample work for those who sought a more impersonal form of domestic service. Many of the females who worked in such establishments were young, aged between 10 and 29 on average.

Not all women in affluent or professional households lived a life of leisure, however – at 9, Bedford Street North, lived Mr Alexander and Mrs Marianna MacIlveen, with sister-in-law Elizabeth and Cousin Alicia, their four daughters, and a 7-year-old visitor, the daughter of an Irish attorney. All the adults are working as teachers – German, French (Marianna and Elizabeth), and Music respectively, presumably at the Mechanics' Institute for which Alexander is head teacher. Two female servants, a cook born in Liverpool and a housemaid born in Bath, make up the rest of the household. The whole household are Irish apart from Alexander, and are a good example of how one must not assume that all Irish-born residents in Liverpool were poor and on a low income – history, being made up of the lives of people, is never that rigidly defined.

Other work available to Liverpool Women

In 1871, 65.7% of women over the age of 20 listed on the census return for Liverpool were still not recorded as having paid work. This was partly because of the port status and the large percentage of low-paid jobs connected with the docks, which were male dominated. In second place was transport-related employment and ocean navigation, again not work normally available to a woman, especially one with a family to look after. Liverpool was known for the fragmented and transitory nature of its work – its 'peculiar irregularity' (Miss Harrison, Liverpool University Jevons scholar, writing in 1907).

However, numerous manufacturing outlets were established, most of them in the second half of the nineteenth century onwards, to process imported raw materials, such as sugar refineries, seedcake mills, cigarette and tobacco factories. Here, females had more opportunities than men, but again, opportunities were restricted due to the nature of trade and industry in the port.

A young woman made the headlines by taking her pet goose with her when she delivered pails of milk in Liverpool. The caption is 'The Goose Step in Liverpool.'

One of the worst dock-related roles was that of the 'bag women', women who undertook the arduous, dirty, abysmally paid work of making and repairing the millions of sacks that carried goods in, around, and out of the port. It was casual work of the least desirable kind, tied to the fluctuations of the dock trade, and it was work done by women with dependants or husbands not working, the Irish, sailor's wives, widows, and older/single women in a desperate attempt to make ends meet. Jute factories bore a similar stigma as did working in rope manufacture, which was also tied to the fluctuations of business connected with the docks, and on busy days women would be expected to work from 6.00 a.m. to 10.00 p.m. The *Married Women's Work* study described women in this work as 'strong in build, rough in type, and inclined to disregard household cleanliness.' Campaigner Mary Bamber tried to encourage these women to organise and fight for better working rights and conditions.

Factory Work

What factory work *was* available to Liverpool women? By far the biggest employer in this area was the tobacco industry, employing 3,000 women by 1900. Cope Brothers, with premises on Paradise Street and later Lord Nelson Street, had been employing women since about 1858 when a strike by male employees left them

Stripping tobacco at the Copes Tobacco Factory, 1892. Copes had a reputation for being a fair employer for its high number of female operatives.

in need of workers, and by 1871 they were employing about 700 women and girls (to 74 males), making them a pioneer of female employment in the tobacco industry. By 1879, the female workforce had doubled, in premises that eventually ran almost the full length of Lord Nelson Street. They favoured 'respectable' women, such as the daughters of shopkeepers and clerical workers. An article in the *English Illustrated Magazine* from 1892 (Vol 9, pp 299-306) presented a utopian description of the factories and the working conditions of the women.

The reader learns about the well-lighted long hall, compared to a girls' college with its rows of 'desks' manned by approximately 200 female workers. This is the cigarette-making hall, where the most skilled work was carried out (there are

Making Cavendish (a type of loose tobacco for pipe smoking) at the Copes Tobacco factory, 1892. Magazine features (from which this sketch is taken) about such companies were a useful way for businesses to promote their product and ethos.

another 400 women on the cigar-making floor). Some women chat quietly, and there is the odd snatch of song. In the corner of the floor is a small inspection room, from which numbered boxes of tobacco are handed out, which each girl makes up and then returns to the inspectors who note the number of completed cigarettes against her records. The average wage is upwards of 15*s* per week, about three-quarters of the income of a skilled male worker. The reporter notes that there are no notices on the walls threatening fines for misdemeanours, and workers who travelled some distance to work could bring food that was cooked for them and served during the allotted break times. Copes were generally regarded as conscientious employers, restricting shifts to between six and eight hours in length (married women were allowed to leave an hour earlier than unmarried women), and offering treats such as Christmas concerts. The article mentions the workers' Benevolent Fund which guaranteed an endowed bed at a local hospital, convalescence by the sea and, for lung conditions, treatment at the Devonshire Hospital in Buxton. The reporter notes the women are soberly dressed, including the ubiquitous Lancashire woollen shawl, and 'every Lancashire girl carries it [the shawl] with grace.' They have personalised their desks with trinkets, and illustrations cut from magazines, and the journalist notes that the tidiest desks, or the most prettily decorated, indicate the most intelligent and attractive girls: 'the desk or table most tastefully arranged will have for its mistress if not a pretty girl then an interesting one, with bright eyes, clean well-cut gown, and hair done up in the latest style of the coiffeur's art. 'Other tasks performed by women at Copes included stripping the tobacco leaves ready for manufacture, spinning tobacco, making Cavendish (a sweet, moist variety of smoking tobacco), and packing the finished cigarettes. In reality, many of the processes involved in the tobacco industry were unpleasant – the spinning of tobacco was carried out in a steam-filled room by gaslight, and much of the work was piece work rather than a set wage. The wage quoted is clearly also a top wage available – apprentice cigar makers started at 2*s* per week.

Cigar making at the Copes Tobacco Factory, 1892. 400 women and girls worked in the cigar making department.

    Other more heavy-handed tobacco manufacturers did not fare so well – Clarke's, based on Richmond Row, was embroiled in an industrial dispute with its largely female workforce in the early 1890s, over draconian fines and low pay. This dispute escalated to a boycott of Clarke's products, organised by the Liverpool Fabians and the Independent Labour Party (ILP). Another important tobacco company was Ogden's, which manufactured Ogden's pipe tobacco, advertised later by the famous billboard with 'real' smoking pipe. Ogden's had begun as a small local business in 1860, and by 1901 had the impressive premises seen in the image on page 49. Like the other tobacco

The most famous BRITISH Cigarette in the World.

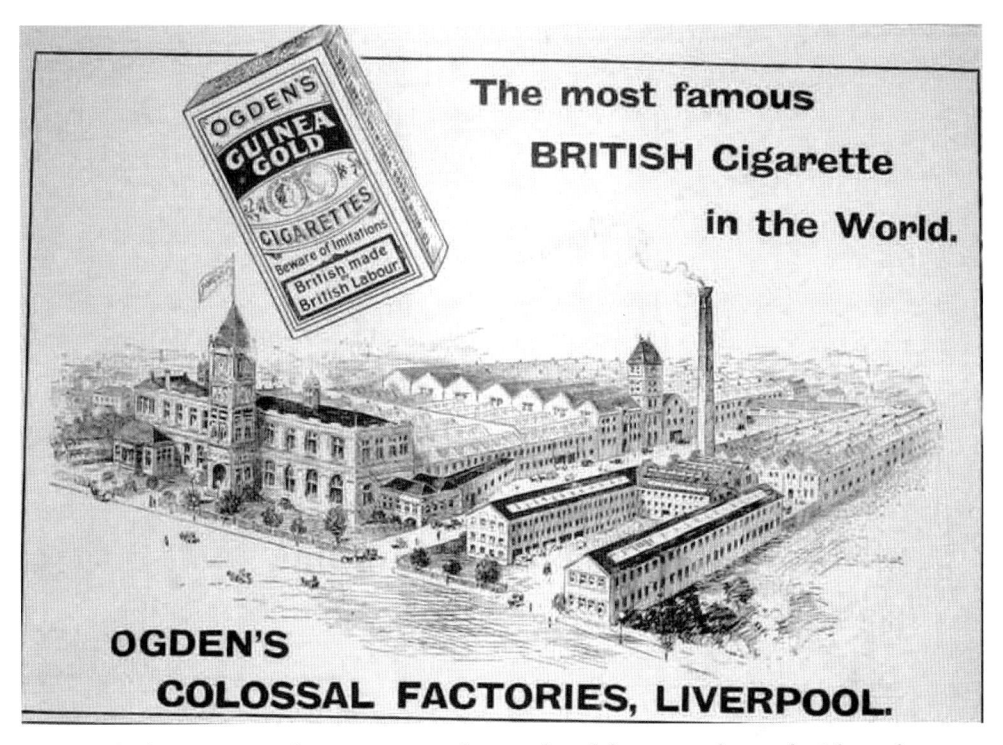

OGDEN'S COLOSSAL FACTORIES, LIVERPOOL.

Ogdens was another company who employed large numbers of girls and women. From 1899 production was based at these new premises in Boundary Lane.

companies, Ogden's employed substantial numbers of women – in the 1920s, the workforce numbered about 3,000.

Jam factory work was popular, as the factories were modern and clean. There was a 'hierarchy' of roles – generally, what were considered to be lower-class women picked over the fruit in the factory before processing, as it was seasonal work and not a reliable source of income. The schedule for a preserves factory included marmalade-making from December to March, rhubarb from May onwards, followed by the summer fruit harvests. Hundreds of women worked in the preserves factories at the height of the season – as many as 600 in the 1890s. A slack time then followed, dominated by pickled-onion-making till about October. Pickling work was not popular, as the smell came out of the factory with the women and it was obvious to everyone where they worked. Other food manufacturers employing significant numbers of women were Crawford's biscuits, and Jacob's biscuits, where women packed loose biscuits into glass-lidded tins which were delivered to grocery shops for customers to create their own 'pick 'n' mix' biscuit assortment. Broken biscuits would be bagged and end up on the market, where frugal homemakers could buy them at a much cheaper price. Wages in the confectionery sector varied from 4*s* to 18*s* per week for the most experienced and quickest workers, in c.1902, with the average wage falling at 8–9*s* per week.

Factory work could be hazardous. Despite the numerous factory Acts passed over the course of the nineteenth and twentieth centuries, industrial injuries were common, and diseases such as TB spread quickly in a closely confined, often dirty and ill-ventilated factory setting. Rope-making (average wage, 6*s* to 12*s* 6*d* per week in c.1902), as at Jackson's ropeworks, resulted in serious injury. One young woman had her fingers torn off by a machine, and in July 1895, Louisa Jane 'Cissy' Muller died a violent and horrific death at the ropeworks when her skirt was caught up in some machinery and she was drawn up to the ceiling and literally torn to pieces. At Cissy's inquest, other stories of injury were related – the woman who was scalped, and another who would have been dragged into a machine and killed had her skirt not given way. It was noted by observers that female factory workers seemed to age quickly, relying on patented medicines and herbal remedies to cope with childbirth (women returned to work as soon as they could after giving birth), minor illnesses, and the all-pervading fatigue of working long hours in a factory and then taking up their traditional role at home afterwards. Cheap pies, hurriedly made stews, and a meal from the fried fish shop sufficed, with pickles to give them extra flavour.

In 1902–3, Liverpool University's Jevons Scholar, Miss A. Harrison, conducted a study of the effects of factory legislation on female workers in Liverpool. She noted the rise of factory employment over the previous half-century, and the increased

WHY BUY NEW?
Velour, Felt, Straw Hats Cleaned or Dyed and Remodelled look and wear like new.

JOHNSONS' DYE WORKS, LIVERPOOL. VELOUR, FELT & STRAW HAT REMODELLING DEPT.

Advertising card for Johnson's Dye Works, Bootle, c.1900. Note the predominance of female staff on the workshop floor – Johnson's employed significant numbers of females.

diversity of work – to the above processes, she adds lead-casting, dyeing and dry-cleaning works (average of 12s per week in 1902), upholstery (average 15s per week following industrial action, c.1902), watch-making, soap-making, and lucifer match-making (employing over 900 females; 5s to approx. 12s per week). The various branches of what she calls the 'hemp industry' – sack-making, jute-spinning and weaving, rope-making, were poorly paid (7s to 10s in c.1902) and out of the nearly ninety per cent female workforce, there was a high proportion of Irish women on the payroll. Those mending sacks on piecework in c.1900 received 1s per hundred sacks. Soap manufacturing offered wages of 8s to 14s in c.1902, with the highest wages going to women who worked piece work, 'dozening' – packing groups of a dozen soaps into a box. One proprietor of a tin-canister factory complained to Harrison that in his opinion, his female workers could earn much more than the average 5–6s per week if they showed more commitment:

> The employer said that if the girls would come regularly they could easily earn from 13s. to 16s. or more. He complained that the girls were satisfied with 8s. a week, and that if a girl made 12s. in one week she would not turn up till the end of the following week. 'If you want them to be regular the only thing to do is to cut them down in wages.'

Harrison also found that employers were reluctant to train young women in better-paid roles, for fear they would marry and have children, and be lost to the workforce. Liverpool was not as well placed to retain married women as other cities such as Manchester, where the textile industry had many thousands of married women working full time.

Married Women and Work

In 1901, 21,457 out of 85,058 women working in Liverpool were married. They found it difficult to work outside the home, but the erratic nature of labouring work in Liverpool meant that women often had to be homemaker and supplement her husband's income as best she could. In the early 1900s, a dock labourer might earn as much as £4 per week by doing overtime, but the 'feast and famine' nature of their work meant overall earnings still averaged out at about £1 per week if they were lucky. Also, the wives of seafaring men often had to go for weeks on end without any money coming in, waiting and coping as best they could by avoiding the rent man, pawning clothes, ornaments and – as a last resort – their wedding ring. Women would help their neighbours out as much as they could, not just out of kindness but with the expectation that when they in turn needed support, it would be readily given. Where there was any money left among friends and neighbours, a 'whip round' might even be possible for the most needy, with people giving whatever coins they could spare despite their own straitened circumstances. The ingenuity of women in this position was remarkable. They could not become live-in domestic servants, because of their own home responsibilities, but there was plenty of charring, kitchen, or cleaning work on a day basis to be had. Many took in work they could do at home: simple home assembly work, such as envelope-making or fancy-box-making, millinery trimmings, needlework, and similar. There were more married women involved in dressmaking and millinery in 1901 than single women, as it was work that could be continued independently at home after marriage and childbearing restricted their opportunities – it also retained many more older women than other part-time or home-based work. In addition, a good worker doing outwork for the tailoring trade could earn decent money, an average of 10–12*s* per week in c.1902. Laundry could be taken in, or children minded. The majority of goods – nearly two-thirds – that were pledged at the pawnbroker on a Monday were usually redeemed by Saturday. Utilising the pawnbroker effectively – there were a plentiful 129 of them in Liverpool in 1885, for example, taking in about 50,000 pledges per week, of which sixty per cent were worth less than five shillings – could be advantageous. Some women would pawn their own clothes, go to the market or second-hand clothes shops, and spend their pawn money on cheap garments such as men's shirts, picking out the ones that were sound enough, but dirty. Back at home, she would give the garments a thorough washing, and then pawn them also for more than they cost, but with no intention of redeeming them. Resourceful women able to manipulate the pawn and credit business in this way had an extra weapon in their fight against poverty and the humiliation of arriving at the workhouse door. Equally, a good relationship with one's local shopkeeper meant a 'slate' could be maintained, allowing for credit in difficult times – although this would have to be carefully managed, as the shopkeeper would not consider extra leeway for any women or family who did not pay off their debt regularly. Street markets offered the opportunity to seek out bargains or goods being sold off because they were 'on the turn', or it was close of business. Failing that, a mother could send her children to scavenge among the litter after the market, looking for scraps that could be flung in the pot at home.

Hawking – taking goods round the streets for low value cash sales – was common, with fruit, matches, 'chips' (wood kindling for fires), and fish being popular choices of 'merchandise'. Children could be taken out into the street with the mother so that she could earn a shilling or two but not have to leave the children to their own devices (or sometimes the children might be sent out to do the hawking alone). Some women left their children with a relative (such as their unemployed husband), as in the example in the Women's Industrial Council study of married women's work, published in 1915 – this mother hawked fruit, to supplement her husband's irregular income, but also because 'she likes the out-door life'. Hawking might raise about 4s per week to add to the family income. Pawning clothes such as petticoats was a common way of obtaining the money to buy goods to stock up their baskets with. A significant minority of female hawkers were also moneylenders, who made loans to other women only if half of it was taken 'in kind' – from her hawker's basket! Thus, a four shilling loan was made up of 2s in cash and 2s worth of fish; Pat O'Mara referred to these 'fish and money women' as 'tough, reckless and morally abandoned.' They also did not take kindly to pedestrians who refused to buy their goods – five women found themselves in trouble for throwing salt and shouting foul language at people in Sawney Pope Street who refused to buy their fish. Other women who went out hawking alone might be using it as a cover for picking pockets, or prostitution. Monsignor Nugent devised a Christmas 'event' to incentivise 'basket women' and hawkers – he offered seasonal treats such as clothing, geese and coal, but only for basket women who could produce a bank book which showed that they had put aside some cash savings in the previous twelve months. Still more poor women bought scraps of rope from marine stores and picked it apart to create 'oakum', used to seal vessels and make them waterproof; oakum picking was cruel to one's hands and the roughness of the rope quickly ripped skin and caused bleeding and infections, all for a tiny profit of a few pennies.

While all this sounds like a hive of small business enterprise, it was often in reality the desperate or last resort of a woman adversely impacted by her husband's or father's precarious work pattern of casual labour, herself then thrown into casual, low-paid work in order to help the family get by – some Liverpool women were contributing as little as 1s 6d per week (about £7.50 today) to the total household income. It was a pattern that could well then be passed down to their children. Poignantly, even among the abjectly poor, there was an element of 'social climbing' – in 1851, a woman in the Scotland Road area described herself as an 'orange dealer', which sounds far too like hawking to be anything else.

The *Married Women's Work* study includes some stark facts about women's contributions to family income. The report focused largely on women who were contributing to a total household income, but widows who were regarded as the main breadwinner are also mentioned in the Liverpool chapter, which concentrated its enquiry on tailoresses, machinists on underclothing (both working at home), women employed in 'bobbin works', and a selection of other occupations – 'jam-making, hair-teasing, bag-mending, sack-sorting'. The samples are anonymous:

– Heavy sewing work (at home): 'A widow, working on corduroy trousers, which she finishes at 2d a pair, earning thereby 8/- a week. Before marriage was a tailoress in a shop, but gave it up "as her children needed attention." Has three children living and has lost six. Takes in a lodger who pays 3/6d; pays 5/6d for five rooms and a kitchen.'
– Factory workers: 'A wife, who does fancy packing (in a sweet factory) at busy season, and gets 8/6d when at work; same trade before marriage. Husband is a crane driver for the Dock Board and gets 25/- to 30/- a week irregularly. She pays 2/6d rent for two rooms, which are clean and tidy, but the furniture is scanty. Has one little boy aged 4 who looks well cared for and healthy. Lost one baby from bronchitis,

whose death the mother attributed to exposure at early and late hours, when she had to take him to the day nursery.'
- 'A woman, employed in a marine store as a rag sorter at 9/- a week; her husband is a casual labourer, out of work; rent 2/- for a half cellar dwelling. Two children of 7 and 5 in a verminous condition; house in a filthy state; the children, she says, "manage for themselves".'

The report comments later in the chapter: 'True it is that sometimes they [the children] have to "manage for themselves", and then we may be sure that we have struck the bed-rock of destitution and despair.'

A solution to unaffordable weekly expenses was to 'downsize' to a smaller dwelling. Families with many children would be crammed into totally unsuitable houses or basements, sleeping two, three or more to a bed, prey to the spread of infectious disease and, as the family was poor, nutrition related problems such as scurvy. An alternative was to take in a lodger, or extended family such as in-laws, and family elders, to help with expenses – this was known as 'huddling'. Bread and oatmeal consumption rose sharply during times of extreme poverty, with even potatoes becoming something of a luxury. Women were particularly vulnerable to nutrition related ailments, due to constant child bearing and everyday drudgery, but also because they went without food themselves in order to see their family fed.

Retail

Women have always been involved in trading, be it a market stall, a hand cart, a basket hawked round the streets, or the interpretation most suited to the nineteenth and twentieth centuries – shops. Annie Garvey, the 'Pier Head Squatter', arrived at Liverpool before 1847 after a particularly rough crossing from Ireland and refused to go another step. She set up a stall on the north west corner of Pier Head, selling apples, oranges, and sundries to the workmen building the Floating Roadway, every day till she died in 1914. As the nineteenth century progressed, more women found work in retail, but the type of retail they engaged in was very varied.

View of Bold Street in the city centre, c.1906. Bold Street was a premier shopping venue for Liverpool people, and several women ran their own businesses here.

A survey of the *1870 Directory of Liverpool* published by Green and Co reveals a wide variety of entries for women, all working on their own account. Many of the businesses are what one might expect – dressmaking and millinery, teachers, launderesses, purveyors of ladies underclothing, baby clothes and hosiery, hairdressers, and stay and corset makers. However, also present are manufacturers (of tallow and grease, and ink), paper dealers, photographers, a medical botanist, pawnbrokers, and French polishers.

Bold Street was one of the leading shopping streets in the city, often selling goods made in their own workshops to the affluent 'carriage trade'. Watch makers, cabinet makers, tailors and gilders all strove to make products that the retail staff – in the early days, almost all male – could easily sell. A survey of the census returns for Bold Street in 1901 also reveals a strong presence by this time of female entrepreneurs. At number 83 lived and worked the 'artist-painter', Elizabeth Smith (b.1865), and her younger sister, and at number 75 was the 'Fancy Work Shop' of Jane Tweddle, a widow, and her daughter Hannah. Janet Drawell kept the tobacconist's shop at number 91, and lived there with her widowed mother and her son, Herbert. At Lloyd's Bank, no. 45, lived widow Charlotte Webster, aged 70, who was the caretaker for the building, with two of her unmarried children; at no. 53 the milliner Helen Cosnette, who was from Cheltenham, lived and worked with her two sisters and a locally born domestic servant.

Work in department stores was highly prized, but in the early days, most retail staff were male, often young, and usually single. Despite the relatively poor pay, this was clean and respectable work, and such young men would have been seen as a good catch for a young woman of similar standing. Liverpool abounded with department stores by the turn of the twentieth century – Lewis's, Owen Owen, Blacklers, Bon Marche, George Henry Lee, Frisby, Dyke and Co, and T.J. Hughes. By the inter-war years, women were a significant percentage of the department

View of Lord Street, c.1907. The emporium Frisby, Dyke & Co employed nineteen female draper's assistants who lived in lodgings on site in 1901.

D. Carter's wool and drapery shop, Bishop Road, Anfield, with proprietor standing outside; c.1950. Female owned or managed shops and small businesses had been a feature of high streets and local shopping parades for over a century, or more.

store workforce, either as shop-floor assistants or in the offices. The stores represented a community all of their own – at Owen Owen, for example, the staff had a swimming club, dramatic society, and annual excursions for the staff to Blackpool or the Lake District. Done in conjunction with T.J. Hughes, these outings represented a huge logistical challenge, with as many as 1,500 staff joining the fun for the day.

The Nursing Profession

Nursing was a female dominated profession, attracting women because it allowed them to use their 'feminine' qualities such as maternalism and nurturing in such a way that their families could not object to the career. The difficulty in the early days was providing adequate training. The Lying-In hospital did attempt to provide training in the 1840s, and in c.1855, a

Nurses' Institute opened in Soho Street. However, once again it was William Rathbone who made the real difference, founding the Liverpool Training School and Home for Nurses. Perhaps coincidentally, also in 1855, the Royal Infirmary began work on a Nurses' Home (see Chapter Two).

After numerous attempts to get the legislation through parliament, the Registration of Nurses Act 1919 came into force, and status of nurses was raised when the General Nursing Council was established which revamped the profession and established rules for entry onto the nurses' register. From this time onwards, nurses had to be of a high standard academically, and as at the time a good secondary or higher education was limited to better-off families, that automatically meant that most nurses came from the middle classes. It took three years' training

EMPLOYMENT BUREAU for EDUCATED WOMEN

14 Colquitt Street, LIVERPOOL.

President—THE COUNTESS OF DERBY.   Chairman—Mrs. F. W. ARCHER.
Hon. Treasurers—{ Mrs. BEATTIE, M.A. AND H. J. FALK, Esq., M.A. }   Secretary—Miss W. K. SALISBURY.
Office Hours : 10.30 to 12.30 and 2 to 4, except Saturdays.
Telephone : Royal 1527

ADVICE and INFORMATION as to openings for Educated Women and the necessary training, are given to Enquirers, and a REGISTER kept of Secretaries, Typists, Matrons, Superintendents, Governesses, Nurses, etc., requiring employment.

As trained workers have a much better chance of obtaining posts, Applicants who wish to train, but cannot afford the necessary fees, are advised to apply for particulars of the **Students' Loan Training Fund.**

Secretarial Training School attached to the Bureau.

"**Women's Employment**," a magazine containing articles on employment topics, and notices of vacant posts, can be obtained at the Bureau (post free 4d.). Prospectus on application.

Fees : Registration, 2/- ; Enquiry, 6d. & 1/-
Suiting 1% on first year's salary.

The Employment Bureau for Educated Women advertising their services in a local directory, 1934. As women came to dominate service roles such as secretarial and clerical work, and telephony, and more single women sought permanent careers, such bureaux proliferated to match applicants with vacancies.

to be registered, with additional training for specialisations, and the profession in the inter-war period was dominated by single women. In 1921, out of the 111,501 nurses, eighty-four per cent were single; in 1931, of 138,670 nurses, eighty-eight per cent were unmarried.

What Women Could or Couldn't Do

There were some occupations which were closed to women, but that did not stop them endeavouring to be a part of that trade. For genuinely male-dominated roles, such as the building trade, or mining later in the nineteenth century, women might pass as male in order to access that work and a man's higher wage. It is hard to say from today's vantage point whether any motivation other than staying out of the workhouse impelled these women to dress and act as a man to do that work, but records do show that some of these women had long-term female partners who even then were referred to as their 'wives'. In 1877, Liverpool cab driver William Seymour was committed for trial on a charge of stealing meat from a butcher's shop in Leece Street. At Walton Gaol the prisoner was found to be female, and transferred to the female wing. Her story, as reported in the *Liverpool Mercury*, was that she was born in Somerset as Mary Honeywell, had married young but unhappily, and had escaped to London. A talented equestrian since childhood, Mary decided to work as a cab driver: 'By wearing her hair short, and by a judicious use of clothing, she managed to present the appearance of a short stout man', especially as she had a face of the 'masculine type'. She worked as a cabbie for six years undetected in Liverpool, living with a woman described as her wife, who brought her lunch to the cab rank every day. Such women are very difficult to trace in the official records, as they almost always have more than one alias – in the case of William/Margaret, the other names are Mary Seymour, Mary Honeywell, and Bill Seymour – there were probably more. In a postscript to this event, Mary/Bill made the newspapers a second time, challenging her mother's will on the grounds of her mother's insanity (she died in the Hampshire

County Asylum). It was reported in the *Belfast Telegraph* that 'the conduct of her family drove the testator mad' (9 November 1877). These 'female husbands' lived always with the threat of exposure, which could destroy a home, long-term partnership, and employment prospects. It was not a decision to be taken lightly, but for those women for whom passing as male was as essential to her projection of self and identity as femininity was to other women, it was not a matter of choice at all.

Well-educated, middle-class women expected to be able to pursue a career or profession if they wished to, especially after the liberating influences of the First World War. The Sex Disqualification (Removal) Act of 1918 stated:

> A person shall not be disqualified by sex or marriage from the exercise of any public function, or from being appointed to or holding any civil or judicial office or post, or from entering or assuming or carrying on any civil profession or vocation, or for admission to any incorporated society (whether incorporated by Royal Charter or otherwise), [and a person shall not be exempted by sex or marriage from the liability to serve as a juror].

In theory, this opened up many professional careers to women, such as the law, although it was not until December 1922 that the first woman was admitted as a solicitor. It also specifically addressed the gender discrimination in the civil service, the courts and the universities. Unfortunately, the Act did not prevent the marriage bar from excluding women from their jobs and careers if they did not remain single. In the years between the two world wars, women in the civil service, teaching and medicine were all affected by this, and for some young women making plans for their life, it must have been a deterrent to even beginning a career, yet ironically, the trauma of so many young, and married, women losing their menfolk to the war had changed the ambitions of many parents for their daughters, and many girls were actively encouraged from now on to 'get on' in the world of work if they could.

Teaching

Teaching has long been a popular career choice for women, and the numerous education Acts generated a need for more teachers that women were eager to fulfil. The 1902 Education Act, which expanded secondary education, was a large part of this process. In 1914 there were already 71,766 female teachers, rising to 120,000 in England and Wales in 1928. During and just after the First World War married women were encouraged to return to teaching, so that by 1921 around one in five women teachers were married. The educational cuts and rising unemployment also moved many local education authorities to introduce marriage bars which led to the sacking of married female teachers in some areas, with decisions based on their husband's income, while others required female teachers to resign on marriage.

The introduction of the Burnham Salaries Scale in the 1920s did help some female teachers, though their wages were often at eighty per cent of men's wages. For women to marry in their twenties after only a few years of teaching was a difficult choice, not only due to the marriage bar. Teachers who had accepted publicly funded grants for training – the majority – were obliged to sign 'The Pledge', whereby they promised to teach for five years after training.

The government's determination to boost the total numbers of available teachers was to backfire; in 1931 there were 132,000 qualified female teachers in Great Britain, and during that decade many found it impossible to get work because supply exceeded demand. By the inter-war period, training took three years for secondary teachers, or two for elementary (primary) teachers; it was possible to be teaching at the age of 18 in an elementary school, having left school at 16 and done one's training. Surveys of middle-class young women in Liverpool showed that many had aspirations to teach as a suitable way of working before marriage.

Unemployment

The options were limited for women with no work, especially the widowed, deserted, or aged and alone. A poor family may do its best to help out, but often they could do nothing at all, as they were struggling to survive themselves. The workhouse was dreaded, but here at least elderly women were not expected to undertake gruellingly heavy work, whereas in the outside world they would certainly be expected to toil until illness and death overtook them. Following the Unemployed Workmen's Act 1905, Distress Committees were set up in Liverpool, which attracted a significant number of female applicants who had tried every means available to get by, but finally had to ask for help. About one third of the unemployed women who came forward were between the ages of 25 and 35; a fifth were aged 15 to 25; and another fifth were 35–45 years. About 400 women per year applied to the committees, most of whom were widows with children who could not take work as domestic servants. About half of the total number were out-of-work charwomen. Many of them wanted cleaning work of a better type – perhaps office cleaning – but the committee could only try to channel a few applicants of good character into sewing work.

Surviving on the Wrong Side of the Law

Some women, either due to the pressures of extreme poverty, abandonment, addiction or illness, or sheer anti-social or sociopathic traits, broke the law to make money or simply to survive. At Walton Gaol in 1861, there were more female committals (4,440) than male (4,419), and by 1873, 6,673 out of 12,420 committals were female. Many women's crimes in Liverpool were relatively petty – disorderliness due to drink, illegal pawning, possession of items that could not be accounted for, prostitution, breach of street-trading regulations, begging and criminal damage. In 1858–9 other crimes included child stealing, assault, robbery on the highway, theft from the person, theft by servants, murder (one case), and keeping disorderly houses. Re-offending rates were high, especially for prostitutes and offences related to alcohol; due to poor supervision, women released early on licence sometimes had little option but to return to their existing criminal circle of acquaintance, which was forbidden under the Habitual Criminals Act 1869. Consequently, some women had more security – and food – when incarcerated, and would commit a petty offence so that they would be sent to prison again. By far the most prodigious offender when it came to petty misdemeanours was Bridget McMullen (b.1843), who, in April 1886, was charged with being drunk and disorderly in a corridor leading to the court, breaking ten panes of glass in the process – she received fourteen days in gaol, but as this was her 113th conviction it is unlikely she was distressed by it. By August of 1888, she had made her 202nd appearance in court. Conditions in Liverpool prisons were often chaotic and undisciplined. In 1895, the governor of Walton prison, Basil Thomson, took a mischievous delight in showing the new Chair of the Prison Commission, Sir Evelyn Ruggles-Brise, a sample of his lively female prisoners. Apparently, Sir Evelyn left the prison ashen-faced.

Gangs in Liverpool also had female members who would commit burglaries and break windows; the gangs often cat-called and jostled female passers-by in the street. Mistresses of gang members were known as Donahs and identified themselves by wearing a certain flower or feather in their hair. They acted as spies, decoys, scouts, and also provided alibis.

One of the most shocking crimes committed by women, was baby farming.

> 'Young couple in comfortable circumstances have a good home for a child … complete surrender, with a premium of £15, would be required.'
>
> (the advertisement used to lure 'clients' in the Smith/Herbert baby farming case, 1907)

To 'farm out' a baby or child meant that the birth parent/s or family were effectively sub-contracting out the role of parent to another, in this case a person who, for a sum of money, would take care of – 'adopt' – the child for the mother on an indefinite basis. Single mothers without family support – 'fallen women' – would make contact with the advertiser and arrange to hand over the child to their safe keeping. The handover often took place in a public place such as a railway station, and the baby farmer would give full assurances to the mother that the baby would be looked after like her own and that regular letters would be sent telling of baby's progress. In most cases there would be little or no further contact between birth mother and child, although the mother would continue to send money for the upkeep of the baby.

Once at the baby farmer's house, the child would more than likely be stripped of its own clothes which would be pawned or sold, placed in a rudimentary bed such as an old drawer, and fed occasionally with a poor mix of artificial food such as cow's milk padded out with completely inappropriate substances such as chalk – and almost invariably laced with an opiate based substance to keep the child quiet. The child would fail to thrive, and die.

Baby farming happened in Liverpool and was widely reported in the local newspapers. The most infamous was the case of Sophia Martha Todd, arrested for the murder of an unnamed infant in 1877. Sophia was the well-educated daughter of an affluent Glasgow engineer. Aged 30 at the time of her downfall, she had ended up in Liverpool after marrying a man named Jackson, but the marriage failed and Sophia had to find her own income. She worked as a bookkeeper in a hotel, but making a living as a single woman at that time was difficult, and at some point she turned to baby farming as a more lucrative alternative. She followed the usual pattern of advertising in the newspaper, and arranging the transaction from there. While lodging with a Miss Joliffe in Prospect Street in 1875, Sophia was seen with a baby she claimed she was minding for a Dr and Mrs George. The child was never seen alive again. Some time later, a mummified child with serious head injuries was found in a clothes box of Sophia's at a different lodgings. By this time she had fled to Old Trafford in Manchester, taken up with a man named Todd and adopted his name; but the police tracked her down and she was brought back to Liverpool to face the allegations of child murder. Sophia was thought to have taken five or more babies plus payment, and the whereabouts of all of them was unknown. Sophia was convicted and received the death sentence, subsequently commuted to life imprisonment, but in July 1883 she was released under licence from Fulham prison, to the care of the Revd James Davidson of St Paul's church in Bristol. From 1882 Sophia had been treated for a number of lung and heart complaints and had been acutely ill, and this seems to be the reason for her release.

Not all infant deaths were the result of a third party, however. Hugh Shimmin revealed that in the year ending 30 June 1862, in Liverpool, inquests were held on eighty-one 'smothered' children, while in 1874, a Liverpool coroner said he thought some parents in Liverpool murdered their children in order to obtain the payout from a Friendly Society; certainly, the practice of 'overlaying' – the suffocation of a baby while lying on it, accidentally or otherwise, at night due to overcrowding or drunkenness, often cited as the reason for a baby's death, was common. Between 1883 and 1888, the Liverpool Society for the Prevention of Cruelty to children noted 700 cases of overlaying, and stated their conviction that a percentage of these would be deliberate; it must be noted that this was not a woman's issue exclusively, it was not always clear how the tragedy had occurred, and social factors must equally be to blame in many cases.

Some women found themselves caught up in crimes as an innocent witness. On 3 August 1874, a Bank Holiday Monday, Alice Morgan witnessed the brutal murder of her husband, Richard, after a trivial argument with a group of males outside the Spruce Beer Shop. When Richard was knocked to the ground and viciously kicked to the stomach and side, Alice tried to protect him and then called for the police. Richard died, and as his coffin was brought out of their home for the funeral, a sympathetic crowd vocalised their support for Alice and their contempt for the murderers – she so moved public opinion with her dignified response to the tragedy that it was even suggested that a fund be set up for her.

Disorderliness was not always born out of criminal intent per se, and sometimes was even an attempt to take the moral high ground, or informally punish or humiliate moral misdemeanours. 'Charivari' or 'rough music', a process by which rowdy groups of people named and shamed adulterers, strike breakers and others considered to have violated unspoken local codes of behaviour, persisted into the mid-nineteenth century. In 1855, Ellen Delaney, aka Kerrigan, gathered together more than twenty female hawkers (not women known for their diffident behaviour) and descended on the home of a woman thought to be having an adulterous affair. Although this was a 'disciplinary' act on behalf of the wronged wife, it degenerated into a riot involving 200 people.

'The Bizzies are after that prozzie!': Sex Workers

('The Police are after that prostitute!' A police officer was also known as a 'slop' or a 'bluebottle')

> It is at night, especially, when the prostitutes [of Liverpool] commence their attack. On Sunday, in particular, they throng out in crowds, almost by main force ... nothing equals the boldness of the Liverpool prostitutes, and the coolness (cynicism) with which they advertise themselves. Nothing is more common than the fights they cause ... [they are] scarcely clothed, disfigured by habitual drunkenness, present a spectacle, the most sad and the most revolting.
>
> (Anon, a physician, from a series of books on the evils of prostitution, *The Greatest of our Social Evils*, writing about prostitution in Liverpool, 1857. See bibliography)

The reasons girls and women resorted to prostitution are familiar – extreme poverty, sole breadwinner for family combined with the abysmal wages for women at that time, addiction challenges; Mgr Nugent also noted the high proportion of orphans in prostitution, and children of first marriages forced out of their homes by a hostile step parent.

Police surgeon Frederick Lowndes took a less empathetic view, citing a love of fine clothes, a lazy nature, and a weakness for alcohol as motivation. It was also suggested that the port status of Liverpool was another reason for the thriving sex trade there, and that when a large number of ships were docked, women even travelled in by train to take advantage of the extra business, while 'floating brothels' moored alongside the ships, each with a brothel keeper on board, to access the business.

There were dozens of brothels in the city throughout the period under study – in c.1850, just five streets in the St John's district had 100 brothels housing 400 prostitutes – this was also known to be a district with high crime rates. Another nine streets in St Bartholomews, St Albans and All Souls had 72 brothels and 280 prostitutes. Prostitutes sought work in cheap theatres, the Zoological Gardens, the Landing Stage, the amphitheatre, or Domville Dance Hall in Lime Street, but the entire waterfront district was probably the most lucrative in terms of steady trade. The Parthenon in Great Charlotte Street was notorious for lewd behaviour and being frequented by large numbers of prostitutes, customers being titillated by *poses plastiques*, similar to a strip show. Of course, by far the simplest method would be to stand on the street and look for custom. Towards the end of the century, soliciting was also common in more distant districts, such as the vicinity of West Derby Road and Walton Road.

Prostitution was a dangerous occupation, and hardly a lucrative living – average prices per client charged by a street prostitute varied from 1*s* to 2*s* 6*d*. Violence, robbery, rape, and the omnipresent threat of sexually transmitted infections (STI) dogged the women every time they worked, and the ready availability of work cannot have been adequate compensation. There was one aspect of prostitution that the establishment was clear about – the notion that prostitutes were solely responsible for the spread of STIs, and that all the men – especially men in the armed forces, and mariners – were the victims of these 'diseased' women, rather than the other way round. The Contagious Diseases Acts of 1864, 1866, and 1868, were intended to give the authorities some control over the sexual health of the army, but in practice gave the police draconian powers to apprehend and detain any woman suspected of soliciting – in fact, any female in the wrong place at the wrong time could be apprehended and expected to submit to an intimate examination by a police doctor, and if she refused she could find herself in prison. Many women were vitriolic in their condemnation of prostitutes – one notable exception was Josephine Butler (1828–1906). A well-educated, strong-minded woman, she was the wife of George Butler, the Headmaster of the Liverpool College for Boys, who took up his post in 1866. He supported her campaign to have the Acts abolished, a campaign which she took around the country and even abroad, and her powerful and persuasive speeches won over people from all classes in society, including Florence Nightingale. Eventually her campaign succeeded, and the Acts were abolished in 1886. Josephine lived for another twenty years, always committed to social activism, taking prostitutes into her home to help them build a new life, visiting workhouses and conducting investigations into deprivation. She supported the pioneering work of others, and visited the reformed infirmary at the city workhouse, impressed by what she saw. In 1920, the Josephine Butler training home was established at 15, Princes Avenue, to train people in social work for vulnerable mothers. The training was thorough for the times, and included physiology, psychology, legal aspects of work, hygiene and domestic economy.

Legalised attacks on women through the Contagious Diseases Acts were more than likely outnumbered by attacks on individual prostitutes. In 1919, prostitute Elizabeth McDermott, aka Isabella Wilson, was found 'stripped of every particle of clothing' (*The Globe*, 27 December 1919), and with her face badly beaten. The *Liverpool Evening News* reported the details of the attack, telling their readers that Elizabeth's corset was pulled off her so violently that it was ripped in two, and that some aspects of the attack were too vile and 'astounding' to be revealed by the newspaper (27 December 1919). She had been killed in a quiet business district in the early hours of Christmas morning, and the various witnesses called on during the investigation revealed an all too familiar lifestyle for a woman of her social and economic status. Elizabeth was a habitual prostitute who had appeared before the magistrates many times, and apparently came from Greenock in Scotland. She told one associate she had been married twice, although by the time of her death she seems to have been isolated from family and long-standing friendships. Elizabeth had recently had an injured shoulder, for which she was treated in the Brownlow Hill Workhouse hospital for six weeks. Her usual abode was a lodging house in Richmond Row, the sort of accommodation frequently used by people struggling to get by. Despite there being at one time two possible suspects, no one was ever convicted of her murder and the case remains unsolved.

Prostitutes were not the only women condemned unfairly when it came to sexuality. The contemporary notion of 'moral miasma', an atmosphere of moral degeneration sometimes generated by cramped and inadequate housing conditions, was thought to lead to incest and the selling of sex. This concept was an extra pressure on women and girls who were already struggling with living conditions that were no fault of their own.

In the inter-war years, recorded prosecutions for soliciting fell markedly, but this does not necessarily suggest a drop in prostitution in the city. Rather, it shows a change in how prostitution was tackled, with social activism leading the way with reform and rehabilitation in the community instead of the more aggressive prosecutions in other large cities such as Manchester. The Liverpool Branch of the Jewish Association for the Protection of Girls and Women and the Liverpool Women's Police Patrol objected to the imprisonment of the women on the grounds that it isolated them from any support they had, such as family, neighbours and the wider community, while prison simply made the women more likely to become habitual offenders, hardened as they were by their experiences in there.

The Development of Clerical Work: 'Office Girls'

One positive effect of the First World War for women was the shift of clerical work from the domain of men, to that of females.

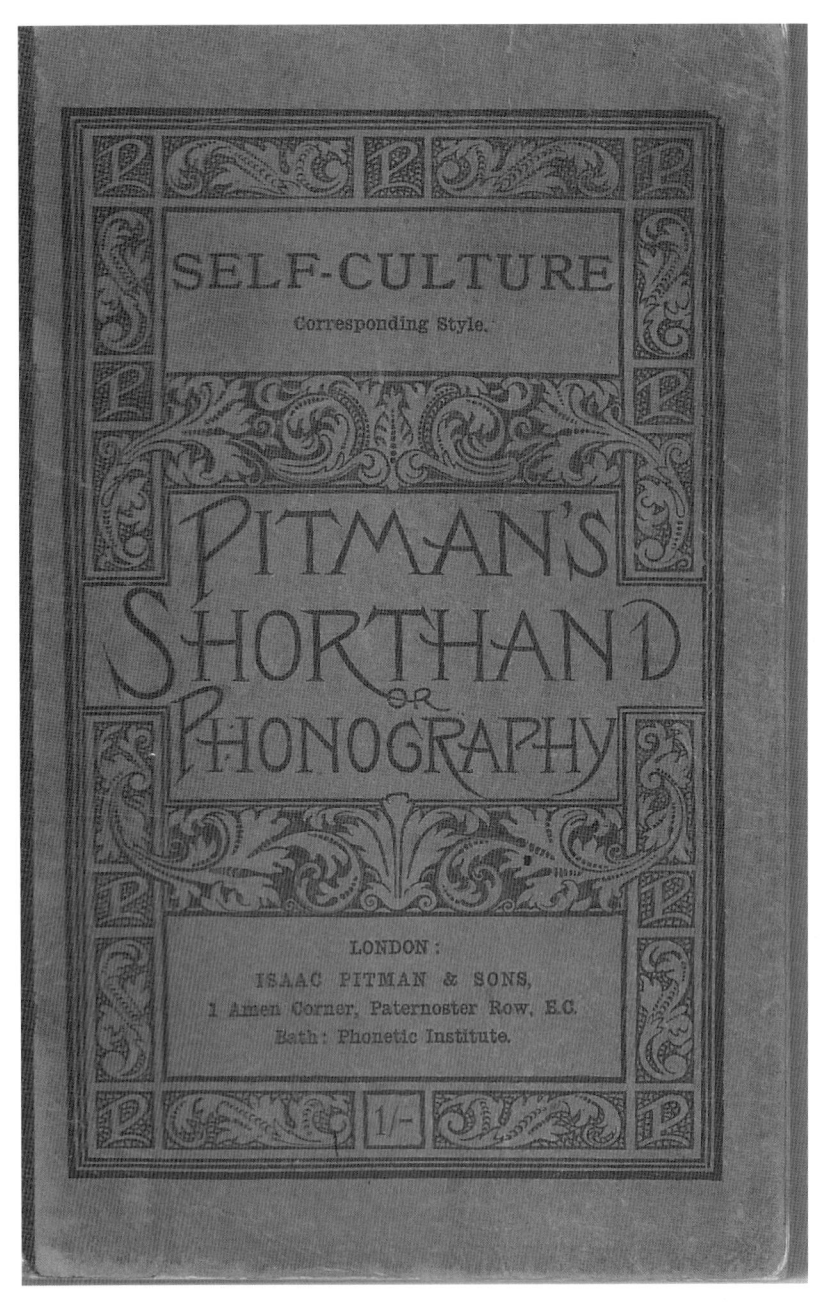

Pitman's shorthand became an essential skill for aspirant secretarial workers, as service industries and clerical workplaces proliferated from the late nineteenth century onwards.

By the mid-1930s in Merseyside, Carradog's Social Survey was reporting that women were working as shorthand typists, bookkeepers, and in various aspects of accounting and invoicing. For unmarried women, local government and the civil service offered a range of opportunities, and full advantage was taken of them. In 1901, women clerks and typists made up ten per cent of the clerical workforce. By 1911 that proportion was seventeen per cent, and by 1921 it was thirty-seven per cent and growing – by the 1920s, working as a shorthand typist or telephonist was regarded as 'women's work'. 'Type writing', as it was originally described, was seen as akin to piano playing, ideally suited to the smaller female fingers. An office was also thought to be a suitable environment for a woman, clean and well ordered, with the genders segregated into different rooms, office suites, or even different floors to avoid any inappropriate behaviour. A strict hierarchy was employed in such offices. Personal secretaries were considered superior to juniors and trainees, and were likely to be middle class with a secondary education, and extensive training in one of the top local secretarial colleges such as Miss Fowke's Secretarial College, learning shorthand, typing, but also business and commercial practice. Next in the hierarchy came girls proficient in typing and copying with some knowledge of business practice – they might have received some training at a lesser secretarial college, such as Marchant and Harpers. Finally, there were teenage working-class women who went straight into office work from elementary education, and received on-the-job training – this was seen as the ideal way for a young girl from a modest background to get a start in a 'respectable' white-collar career, with the possibility of advancement and a 'better' marriage. Pitman was virtually universal as the form of shorthand to learn, and the manual illustrated was specifically designed for use as a home study course, enabling women to study to improve their prospects while working in another form of employment. Undoubtedly, the large number of clerical jobs now available to women after 1918 contributed towards a higher than average level of female employment in Liverpool, despite the growing pressure to return solely to their pre-war domestic duties, and an increasing trend towards giving up work on marriage.

Betterment for aspirant office workers sometimes came in different forms. In the mid-1930s, teenager Dora Davenport was working at Littlewood's, the football pools and mail order company founded by John Moores Snr (1896–1993). As one of the lift girls, it was a humble start to her business career, sitting all day on a tiny drop-down seat in the corner of the lift, operating the controls to take it from floor to floor. A younger member of a large family, raised by her widowed mother, Dora was ambitious to do better for herself and to help her family; when not operating the lift, she studied her Pitman shorthand manuals for the evening class she had enrolled on. Dora left school at 14 and did not want factory work – office work was a career that was within reach if a girl like her made enough effort. One morning, John Moores himself, by then a millionaire, stepped into the lift with a colleague and spotted Dora's books, tucked into the corner. 'What are you reading?' he asked. Dora explained that she was studying a Pitman course, to pursue her dream of becoming a shorthand-typist. 'So you're not happy in this job, then?' he asked her. 'Yes I am', Dora assured him, 'But I know I can do much better than this.' This must have touched a chord with Moores, a self-made man who understood that hard work could bring rewards for a person from humble beginnings. He thought about it for a moment and replied, 'All right then, leave it with me – before I have lunch I'll go up and see the supervisor in the typing pool.' Moores was a good as his word, and soon Dora had her cherished role as a shorthand-typist for the company.

'For the Duration': The First World War, 1914–1918

After the outbreak of war on 4 August, 1914, Liverpool started to feel the shortage of male labour. The answer was obvious, if not universally popular: put the nation's women to work 'for the duration' of the war, on the understanding they would relinquish those roles as soon as the conflict was over. Some areas of work successfully resisted the female workforce, such as the docks – there were moves in 1916 to have female porters, but this was defeated by the dock labourers' union. The James Troop brass foundry on Pleasant Hill Street was involved in aircraft making and took on female employees. Many women chose to use the skills honed in housewifery and family care to become Voluntary Aid Detachment (VAD) nurses, supporting the trained medical and nursing staff in voluntary military hospitals, although there was some resentment from the trained nurses when it was thought that the VADs were classing themselves as professional nurses too. Middle-class women in particular benefited from war work, as they almost always gave up work on marriage, and this was an opportunity for them to alleviate boredom, isolation and loneliness, and to experience again the camaraderie and fulfilment of the workplace.

The increasingly violent campaign for women's suffrage all but ground to a halt during the war. The Women's Social and Political Union (WSPU) officially ceased activities, and the Liverpool branch ended in the September. Some suffrage groups, such as the Women's Freedom League and the United Suffragists, managed to keep going, and some women wanted to support the war effort and keep their suffrage activism going at the same time, while others simply stopped campaigning altogether, using skills honed in suffrage campaigning to help the war effort in some way – it did not feel like the right time to deepen divisions between the genders. Ironically, the cautious Eleanor Rathbone warned against the complete abandonment of their old campaigns, as it would set back the entry of women into public life in the long run. Sewing and knitting, social activism among servicemen's families, and moral patrols were popular choices of activity among these able women. Cicely Leadley-Brown set up the Patriotic Housekeeping Scheme, with an exhibition held in Liverpool in 1915, which offered meatless frugal cookery demonstrations, shoe repairing and child welfare advice.

Phyllis Lovell, a suffragette who claimed to have militant credentials, formed the Home Service Corps (HSC) in 1914 – she wanted to show that if women could commit themselves to public duty, and show discipline and female unity in the face of war, then they could use a vote in a responsible manner. She was aided by close colleagues, such as Mrs Stanley Clarke. The HSC was a rigidly disciplined civilian service (see page 77, Lovell putting some recruits through their drill), and the members wore a navy uniform with cap. The women were not only drilled but highly organised, with local branches and their own newsletter, the *Home Service Corps Review*. It was a resounding success compared to the national women's reserve that was established in 1915 – 2,000 women came forward to sign up for the HSC, but only 300 for the national reserve, in Liverpool. From their HQ in Church Street, the HSC ran classes in horse- and motor-driving, gardening, and bookkeeping. Some women did less exciting work, such as operating lifts, but still did the work with military precision and pride.

Other women did work unheard of before the war began – they became part of the Police Aid Detachment (PAD). The PAD was established at the request of the Chief Constable of Lancashire in 1915, and began by patrolling parks and policing free concerts given for the troops. By 1916, some of the female officers were undertaking detective work, and so impressed was the Watch Committee in Birkenhead that they set up the country's first official female police force in 1917. Lovell was Sergeant in Charge of the forty women, and wrote of her enormous pride in her healthy young officers. It was not all plain sailing, however – Lovell resigned her police commission in protest over not being allowed powers of arrest.

Two other organisations contributed to the war effort but in a less militaristic way – the Women's War Service Bureau (WWSB) and the Ladies Branch of the Civil Service League (CSL; established 1911). Whereas Phyllis Lovell had used the HSC to promote gender equality, the other two groups emphasised 'unique' feminine qualities women had, such as nurturing and caring. The CSL was small in scale as membership was limited to 100, but it did offer ambulance classes and secretarial training, and made bandages, food parcels and clothing to be sent to the front-line troops. The WWSB had eminently respectable

Miss Phyllis Lovell putting a group of First World War female volunteers through their drill in Liverpool, c.1914-15. A militant suffragist, Lovell was involved in numerous very active women's organizations which promoted female participation in the war effort whilst also maintaining calls for full citizenship rights for women.

beginnings. The Lady Mayoress, Mrs Herbert Rathbone, had called for women to come forward at the start of the war to help the war effort. Her call was promptly answered by Dr Mary Davies of the NUWSS, and eventually, the leadership of the WWSB was peopled by numerous ex-NUWSS members such as Edith Bright. Dr Davies had been offered a house in Gambier Terrace for the war effort and this became the WWSB HQ. Sadly, the two organisations were uneasy rivals, but eventually the CSl was offered a room at Gambier Terrace in an attempt to promote a better relationship between the two. Like the CSL, the WWSB made food parcels and collected clothing for the troops, and it also organised the Soldiers' and Sailors' Families Association, responsible for distributing 'service separation allowances' to the servicemen's wives, which varied according to the size of the family. The association also ran social clubs for the wives of servicemen, where they could have friendship and support.

The poor of Liverpool suffered even more during the war partly due to inflation, and the United Suffragists (US) stepped in to help by organising a clothing bureau to make sure nobody went without warm clothing. The WWSB also contributed to the Women's Patrols (a national initiative by the National Union of Women Workers), which were primarily concerned with the moral welfare of females. There was no uniform, just a simple armband, and their ambitions went no further than a protective desire to remove females and children from potential harm. Concerns for the moral welfare of the city's women were high as thousands of troops were stationed nearby, and some even called for a return to the Contagious Diseases Acts. Many young women went to the soldiers' camps, and it was felt necessary to have welfare patrols to protect the women from themselves and the men they socialised with, offering them wholesome entertainment at social clubs instead. It is not known how popular the female-only clubs were. The patrols also kept a close eye on Liverpool's street social life, and they visited the homes of young women known to the police to talk to them about their behaviour. The patrols only engaged women over the age of 27, whilst Phyllis Lovell's police patrols were initially all women under the age of 30, 'healthy and of good physique', reported Lovell proudly.

The war created the inevitable result of all conflicts – 13,500 Liverpudlian casualties, and many newly created widows and orphans. At the end of the war, women once vital to the war effort were sent back to their homes and families, but some had no opportunity to create their own family – their husband or fiancé was dead. The so-called 'reward' of enfranchisement at the end of the war in exchange for women's war work, for many, was too high a price to pay.

'Just give me five minutes with that man!' The Second World War, 1939–1945

(The words of Miss Scott, head teacher in Liverpool, about Adolf Hitler, the night before her school was evacuated from Liverpool to Shrewsbury on 3 September 1939; Mass Observation Archive: from the diary of Miss Mary Pickles, teacher)

As a port, Liverpool took a heavy punishment during the Second World War, with the highest number of casualties of any city outside London – over just two days alone during the Liverpool Blitz, 20 to 22 December 1940, 500 enemy aircraft concentrated their attack on the city. In 1941, over the first seven days of May, 800 enemy planes attacked the city, with familiar landmarks such as the central library, Lord Street, and the Blue Coat School hit; the resulting fires could be seen in North Wales, Cheshire and South Lancashire. On a domestic level, many women and their families lost their homes. Of the 282,000 homes in the city, 184,840 were damaged in bombing raids, and 10,840 were destroyed. No building was safe – in December 1940, the Mill Road Nurses' Home was hit by a stray bomb, but thankfully there were no casualties, as the nurses were in the shelters at the front of the building. The following May, Mill Road hospital took a direct hit – in the maternity ward, mothers and babies were killed along with two midwives; elsewhere in Mill Road more patients died, and two nurses in the operating theatre.

It was because of the fear of such bombings that evacuations of the young, elderly, and vulnerable began. The evacuation of children caused many mothers untold distress. It began 1 September, and continued sporadically throughout the war thereafter, with further evacuations in 1941 and 1944. Children were sent considerable distances – Herefordshire, Shropshire, all parts of North Wales, and closer to home, rural Cheshire and Southport. On 4 December 1939, the *Liverpool Daily Post* reported that there were still 43,400 Liverpool children in the reception areas, but some had already been collected by distraught parents who decided that they would face whatever perils were to come with their children by their side, united as a family. Parents were expected to contribute towards the cost of the evacuation and a child's board at their temporary home, up to a cost of 9s per week per child. The same issue of the *Daily Post* noted with satisfaction that 'Liverpool parents, even the poorest, have responded very well from the beginning, and they regularly attend the fifteen or sixteen centres, on Saturdays and Mondays, to hand over their shillings.' Of the 95,000 evacuees in 1939, 57,000 were school children, and 31,000 were mothers with children under the age of 5.

Not all evacuation was outwards, however – following the evacuation of Gibraltar in 1940, 12,000 women and children arrived in Liverpool early in the war, and in 1944, the Liverpool WVS received 861 children and mothers from the vicinity of Woolwich in Kent – the women volunteers worked through the night to feed and bathe the children, and find suitable billets for them.

The war enabled some women to access employment of a new and interesting – even exciting and secret – kind, while married women who had not worked for many years suddenly found their skills in demand again, as in the teaching profession. Other women, such as Dora Davenport, lost their jobs, but in Dora's case she was not prepared to give in to the loss without a fight.

In 1939, it was thought inappropriate to squander money through betting games such as the football pools, and the machinery and buildings were required for war work, so the pools operation at Littlewood's was repurposed. The printing side of Littlewoods, J&C Moores, was turned over to printing the National Registration cards so important to each citizen – without a National Registration number, one could not have a ration book. This was a brisk start to Liverpool's civilian war effort, but it also resulted in thousands of women losing their jobs altogether, the huge offices of pools checkers and those in related roles were suddenly unemployed. Dora and three colleagues, May Edge, Lily Samuels, and Myrtle Brown, with the help of other redundant women, distributed leaflets outside the labour exchanges to those affected, inviting them to meet at the WEA (Worker's Educational Association) Rooms in Hope Street.

The response was overwhelming, with so many women turning up that they could not all fit into the venue. A lively discussion followed, with some suggesting that they be trained as ambulance or lorry drivers in connection with air raid precaution work, or that overtime in factories should be banned to make room for more workers; it was also suggested that 'inefficient society lovelies' who didn't need the money should be made to relinquish their posts in favour of working-class women who would do a much better job. (*Liverpool Daily Post*, 14 November 1939). The campaign adopted the slogan 'We Want Work'. It was agreed to petition the Lord Mayor, Sydney Jones, to accept a deputation of the women to present their grievances. On 3 December another meeting was held, this time at Picton Hall, chaired by Lily Samuels, and a resolution was passed to keep fighting until every woman affected had work; they also planned to organise a deputation to the Minister for Labour, Ernest Brown. Lily Samuels told the meeting that a letter of support had been received from Ellen Wilkinson, a noted campaigning MP, the Trade Union Youth Advisory Council, and the Liverpool University Socialist Society. Dora Davenport spoke next, criticising the local labour exchanges for failing to find work for the redundant women, and acknowledged that of course football pools was gambling, but as far as the women were concerned, it was their good honest hard work that had contributed to the success of the company in the first place. She continued:

> We are not just trying to be awkward, we are in desperate need of work…We do not want to face the blackest Christmas of our lives. Many people are feeling the pinch in this war, but for us the pinch has been a darned big bite. We do not mind whether we work on guns or coupons, provided we are sufficiently paid.
>
> (*Liverpool Daily Post*, 4 December 1939)

May Edge also spoke, claiming that the war had created more unemployment among women generally than among men. Other speakers included Jack Braddock, husband of Bessie Braddock who was by then a noted local politician (see Chapter Seven). Later in the month, two of the campaigners travelled to London and, before addressing a conference of the British Youth Peace Assembly, called at Downing Street and left a calling card with an appeal to Prime Minister Neville Chamberlain to donate to the relief fund for the unemployed pools workers.

It is not known how the many hundreds of Littlewoods women fared in the war with their work situations. Perhaps some were taken back, as the company turned its formidable resources to war work, making barrage balloons (1940 onwards), dinghies and munitions (1941 onwards), and aircraft parts (1942 onwards), tasks well suited to either male or female workers. Other women preferred to support the war effort 'on the home front', and were actively encouraged by every media. The Will's cigarette company issued a new set of fifty collectible cards entitled *Air Raid Precautions.* Avidly collected by many children and adults, about one quarter of the set included images of women trying on gas masks, fire fighting, and operating ventilation machines for gas-proof chambers – tasks such as operating anti-aircraft guns were reserved for men. This and other popular forms of propaganda – women's magazines, movies, and popular music – accustomed the population to the idea of women mobilising yet again after facing a push-back into the domestic sphere in the inter-war period. As a result, women responded well to appeals for their contribution, and in 1941 the *Liverpool Daily Post* reported that 400 women had just signed on at the Leece Street Labour Exchange alone (11 September).

The Compulsory Fire Watching Order for Women, came into force on 14 September 1942, compelling adult females between the ages of 20 and 45 who did not have children under the age of 14, to do their share of the fire watching. However, a significant number of women did not come forward to enlist. An article in the *Liverpool Echo* (13 October 1942) outlined a broadening of opportunities to do so, allowing women 'who, for various reasons such as sickness, working late and temporary absence from the city have been prevented from registering.' By 1943, concerns were continually raised about women on fire guard duties in 'vulnerable parts of the city' (*Liverpool Echo*, 31 December 1943) close to the River Mersey, with unsafe buildings; after a meeting between Liverpool MPs including Ellen Wilkinson, and the Liverpool Civil Defence Emergency Committee, it was decreed that women would only be required to perform Fire Guard duties (if at all) where they worked, and a determination was expressed that women must have access to suitable facilities such as adequate sleeping arrangements. There was bickering in the letters pages of the local press, one man writing in to state his opinion that 'the agitation for many years now has been that women can do the same work as men. Now that fire watching has arisen a great many seem to have suddenly changed their views', and pointing out that Russian women did all manner of heavy work 'and no squealing either'. (*Liverpool Echo* 4 September 1942)

In the same issue, 'Woman Air Warden' wrote: 'I have nothing but admiration of, and pride in, the women wardens ... I know of no single instance of a woman failing to carry out her duties night after night during the worst of the raids.' Men denounced the compulsory nature of fire watching, demanding that capitalists return from their Lake District or North Wales country homes to do their own fire watching instead of expecting women to do it, and others flatly refusing to allow their daughters to undertake such potentially dangerous work. It was not all danger, however – on quiet nights, women could knit 'comforts' for those in the armed services. The Royal Air Force Comforts Committee would send 2lbs of knitting wool and a pattern book so the recipient could make regulation style pullovers, scarves, gloves and so on. The finished items were mailed back to London for distribution. Those women who were adept at making their own clothes would unpick knitted garments and remake them; one young woman even made herself a Fair Isle sweater out of different coloured darning wools. 'Make do and mend' extended to sewing too, but for those who wanted a treat or were not good at dressmaking, a visit to C&A Modes would offer a choice of 'Utility' frocks – different colours, but all the same style. Queues were everywhere, for all manner of goods, and some women would plant themselves in one queue and place their older children in other queues, in order to have the best chance of obtaining supplies.

For women who continued in factory work, or were assigned to it during the war, the vast majority of companies were turned over to war requirements. The Royal Ordnance Factory in Kirkby worked shifts round the clock – night shifts paid £5 per week, and days, £3 per week. It was not an easy place to work, with numerous accidents and even a fatality.

Some women left Liverpool altogether, enlisting in the armed forces and coming home on leave when allowed, on train journeys delayed by hours, travelling at a tortuously slow speed through stations devoid of name plates, and subject to blackout regulations in the carriages. Other women came to Liverpool for the first time, posted there to join in the war effort. One such

'WRNS' (Women's Royal Naval Service) in rare moments of leisure in Greenbank Gardens, Greenbank House, 1944. Details of picture to the left: from left to right, starting at rear: Mavis, Moira, 'Pargie' (the author Edith Pargeter/ Ellis Peters), Merle, (not known), Jean, Mollie. Details of picture to the right: from left to right, starting at rear: Cath, Moira, Mollie, (not known).

young woman was Edith Pargeter (1913–1995), later known as the author of the medieval *Cadfael* novels using her pen name Ellis Peters. This unassuming young woman was working in a chemist's shop in her home county of Shropshire when the war began, but was also a published writer by this time; she enlisted in the WRNS in 1940 and, thanks to her typewriting skills, she was assigned as a teleprinter operator. Initially stationed at Devonport as part of the joint Plymouth and Western Approaches command, after the two commands split in 1941, she was one of the personnel moved to Liverpool to work in new Western Approaches HQ at Derby House, Rumford Street, under the command of Admiral Sir Percy Noble. Liverpool received 1,000 convoys during the war, so it was the ideal location for such a mission. From this specially strengthened building, naval and air forces were coordinated twenty-four hours a day by up to 400 men and women, with some of Edith's female colleagues moving the wooden pieces representing the ships on a huge map of the ocean. Edith may have been billeted at Greenwood House, the former home of the Rathbones which had been gifted to the city, or nearby Westfield; certainly, she and her friends in the service used Greenbank Park for much needed leisure. Throughout the war 'Pargie', as she was known, continued to write, and in 1942 published *She Went to War*, a novel in the epistolary style telling the story of a young woman who joins the WRNS and is posted to Liverpool. Pargeter later revealed that the background setting of the story was taken directly from her observations of the war around her as it was happening in Liverpool, and it gives wonderfully vivid insights into her life there. Here, she describes a night in a bomb shelter:

> Eighty or ninety girls in pyjamas, blankets, travelling-rugs, eiderdowns, greatcoats, scarves, their hair in curlers under giddy chiffon handkerchiefs, their faces greased and glistening with cold cream; and all these girls crammed into two or three small rooms … entangled in one another's knitting and embarrassed by one another's looks.

Two views of Greenbank House, 1944. The property, originally owned by the Rathbone family, was used as WRNS quarters during the latter part of the Second World War.

In the billet, Pargie would have shared a room with a dozen women, perhaps more, and was ideally placed to observe and remember their stories and routines. At work, she was known to be a diligent and able worker, and by the time she was awarded the British Empire Medal on 1 January 1944, she had attained the rank of Petty Officer. After demob, Pargie returned to her beloved Shropshire, and continued with her writing career to great acclaim, one of many thousands of women in both war and peace who had a significant impact on the life of Liverpool.

Men and women who had toiled in long shifts needed a social outlet. Theatres and cinemas continued to be popular, with most people choosing the matinee if they could, to avoid the blackout, while pubs, cafes and restaurants served the best fare they could within the food restrictions. The Grafton was packed during the war, a magnet for servicemen of all nationalities. Some servicemen, notably the American GIs, were invited to the homes of local families, and appreciated the kindness and hospitality they encountered there. In return, the US Army provided Christmas parcels of sweets and biscuits for thousands of sick and orphaned children in Liverpool in 1944. While the vast majority of contact between local women and American soldiers was amicable and sometimes romantic, a few isolated cases of sexual assault did come to light. In October 1942, 34-year-old Ellen Rigby was subjected to a two-hour sexual ordeal by an American soldier after being pulled from her bicycle in Maghull and into a nearby field. The soldier received a life sentence for his crime, and Ellen, who had had no previous sexual experience, became pregnant and gave birth to a son the following year.

CHAPTER FOUR

'Sagging Off with a Sprowser in Me Pocket': Education

✦

(Translation: 'Playing truant from school with a sixpenny piece [pre-decimal money] in my pocket')

Introduction

In the years leading up to 1850, only about half of all Liverpool's girls could read or write. This is no reflection on their abilities – there was no universal education for children, and not all families took advantage of the basic education offered by Sunday schools. Not until the 1870 Education Act, did all working-class children have the chance to be educated. Local school boards were elected which established elementary schools within their area of responsibility, and two women – Florence Melly and Ann Jane Davies, served in Liverpool from its beginnings. However, this Act only established the principle of universal education, and another Education Act in 1880 was required to make that education compulsory. Not all mothers appreciated the value of such education, especially for daughters, as they were used to having children at home to help with chores, or to watch the younger children while the mother worked, and women who did outworking also wanted their children at home to help with that, to earn a few extra pennies. Many families felt that all a girl needed to know was how to be a good wife and mother, and run a home to an adequate standard. Reliance on the help of children in the home was such an accepted part of working-class family life that only a change in the law, with penalties for transgressions, would put an end to the practice – although many of a girl's domestic responsibilities were simply moved to the few hours after school, when she got home. Following the 1902 Education Act, schools moved to local authority control, and in 1918, the compulsory school leaving age was raised to 14 for all children. Even in the 1930s, local toy companies in the twentieth century exploited the cultural pressure on girls, with adverts such as that for the Dolly Varden folding doll's house. Here, two happy little girls literally 'play house', and real children could have specially made furniture to arrange tastefully inside it. The 1948 act widened provision again, with universal secondary education for all children. Children in the workhouse also had a school to attend.

c.1936: two little girls are depicted playing happily with this locally made Meccano 'Dolly Varden' folding doll's house. Toys such as this were seen as ideal for girls and would teach housewifery and female-oriented roles seen as useful in their adult life.

Schools

Of course, those with the money to spare had always had the opportunity to educate their children. From 1888 onwards, girls could attend Merchant Taylors' School for Girls in Crosby, while The Liverpool High School (part of the Girls' Public Day School Trust) opened in Prince's Park in 1880, and in 1911 changed its name to The Belvedere School, in order to stand out from other high schools in the area. In the 1890s, a private school was charging well over two guineas per term to educate girls:

LIVERPOOL INSTITUTE, MOUNT STREET
(Founded 1825)

HIGH SCHOOL FOR GIRLS (Blackburn House)

£1.8s – £2.18s. Per Term.

(*Liverpool Mercury*, 15 April 1895)

c.1925: a group of older Liverpool school girls dressed as 'pierrettes' show off their combined dance and exercise display. The girl to the extreme left is believed to be Veronica McDonnelly.

In the same newspaper, the East Liverpool High School for Girls was advertising for pupils for the new term. Based at 83 Newsham Drive, the head teacher was a Miss Silcox. The school also had a preparatory department. Codes of conduct at many of the girls' schools were rigorously applied. The head teacher of Merchant Taylors' in the inter-war period, Miss Fordham, was apparently known for cruising round in a taxi after school hours to ensure that no girls were breaking the rule of not talking to boys in public while wearing school uniform!

Later on, grammar schools such as Holly Lodge, St Edmund's College, and Aigburgh Vale drew on local catchment areas, and the private convent school, Seafield in Crosby, offered a less rigorous and more faith based option.

The vast majority of privately educated, middle-class girls did not leave school until they were 18. When a girl had finished her school education, she could go on to a private college if she wished and her parents were willing to pay. The F. L. Calder College of Domestic Science in Colquitt Street offered courses in housewifery (literally, learning how to be a housewife and run a home efficiently) and domestic science. A one year course in housewifery was ideal for those who simply wanted to learn how to run their home, and more intensive courses qualified the student to teach domestic science herself.

Higher Education

As early as the 1860s, there were campaigns to pioneer higher education for women in Liverpool. Anne Clough founded the Liverpool Ladies Education Association in 1866, and in 1874, the Association to Promote Higher Education was founded in the city at a meeting addressed by William Rathbone and Emily Davies, one of the pioneers of women's education in Britain and first Principal of Girton College, Cambridge. The association ran over forty courses to prepare students for the Cambridge Extension Scheme certificate.

In order to go to university, the aspirant scholar had to stay on at school till she was 18, and complete her Higher School

Certificate. Should she wish to stay local, Liverpool University, a well respected 'red brick' university (one of the nine civic universities founded in major industrial centres in the nineteenth century) had admitted its first eighteen women to the University College in January 1882. Some were as young as 16; entry at 15 was permitted for students after tests in a language (Greek, Latin or French), Maths and Science and if their teachers were willing to support their application. By the late 1880s there were nearly fifty female students, sixty in 1892, and seventy-five in 1896. Enrolments were made each term, with the majority studying towards Junior or Intermediate levels of awards in London or Cambridge Local Examinations.

At first, the college did not offer degrees, and when it did it was as a constituent member of Victoria University. Elizabeth Becket took a degree in Greek, while other students awarded degrees in the late 1880s include Mary Burn (BA), and Ellen

The University College, later the University of Liverpool, c.1900. The college accepted female students from as early as 1882 – although initially, all their lecturers were male.

McConnell (BA), and Jessie Auld (BSc). Most of the female students would have chosen subjects such as Art, Natural History, Languages (Greek, Latin, Italian, German and French), Economics, History, Classics, English Language and Literature, Philosophy or Mathematics. It is not known how many women studied Chemistry, Physics or Engineering at this time. The college became the University of Liverpool in 1903. Student life for these women was clearly a stimulating and liberating experience, and from the early days they had their own student bodies. The Women's Student Council, formed in 1886, organised the Women's Common Room and reading room and their facilities, and in 1887, the Women's Literary Society had fifty members.

Local female students often lived at home, but in 1899 a women's Hall of Residence was provided by Emma Holt at a house in Edge Lane and later at Fairfield. A clubhouse for them was located at 28 Brownlow Street from 1896 before the Students' Union Building was erected in 1911. Many social events took place in the Victoria Building, either in the entrance hall or the lecture theatre, a popular venue for 'Smoking Concerts', musical evenings and theatricals. Sports facilities at this time were provided in Wavertree, Knotty Ash, Penny Lane and Calderstones, until the Wyncote Estate in Allerton was bought in 1920. However, a note of caution must be added here regarding the freedom of women to join in all the activities. As late as the 1930s, females were excluded from some university clubs and social events, but would have had the company of each other and it was probably a blessing in disguise that they had fewer distractions than the male students.

What do we know of the women who pioneered undergraduate studies in Liverpool? One example is Jessie Auld, BSc. She was born in Liverpool to Scottish parents, James and Ellen Auld – James was a distiller's accountant in 1881, when the family were living in York Villas, Everton, and at that time, Jessie was 11 years old – all her siblings were also born in Liverpool. She graduated at the astonishing age of 18, a remarkable achievement. By the age of 21 she was listed on the 1891 census as a 'teacher of mathematics and chemistry' at Weirfield School in Taunton,

A sketch of the Reilly Building, University of Liverpool, c.1920, printed to raise money for the fund raising appeal. Captioned 'Woman's Union,' it represents the wide variety of facilities available to female students from the early days of the university college.

Somerset, a small school for teenage girls with twenty students under the joint headship of Mr and Mrs Loveday. By the 1901 census, Jessie had moved back north and was a resident teacher at Baliol School in Sedburgh, an imposing stone building in its own grounds. It was a girls' school established in 1900, and with reference to women's sports at that time (see Chapter Five), the school had a cricket team as early as 1902, when they played a match against Sedburgh Ladies.

In 1911 Jessie is enumerated not at a school, but is in Church Stretton, Shropshire, at the market garden of proprietors Lucie Barrett and Amy D'Ormieux Boswell, young women in their mid-twenties. Curiously, Jessie is listed as a 'gardening pupil' to the two women, learning the trade of market gardening. She is now 41 years old and has been studying hard or teaching since her mid-teens. Is she staying with friends or even former scholars from her work, and the 'pupil' reference is a joke on their part? There is no immediate evidence to support this theory, although Amy is of equal social standing to Jessie, being the daughter of a surgeon. Could this then be this some form of mid-life crisis and Jessie had turned her back on academia to live in the countryside and grow plants – or is she simply spending an Easter holiday in the countryside?

Jessie did not remain in the Shropshire countryside. In the 1939 National Register, she is residing at 1, Baliol Cottage, Joss Lane, Sedburgh. Baliol School had closed in 1932, and she is listed as a retired teacher, and is living with Catherine Gordon, another retired teacher eighteen years her junior. Set in almost perfect rolling countryside, Jessie must have read with horror and dismay the accounts of the Blitz in her home city of Liverpool, the worst of which was in 1941, and it must have felt like a different world to the quiet environment in which she had chosen to settle, even though her old school, Baliol, was used as a military training school during the war.

Jessie died in 1953, aged 84, and two of her executors were her spinster sisters, Catherine and Lilian. Lilian had become a teacher herself, at secondary level, as had Muriel, another younger sister, who on the 1881 census was as yet an unnamed new-born baby – although Muriel made it to headmistress. In the 1939 Register, Lilian and Muriel are retired and living together in Barrow-in-Furness. Out of a family that included six daughters, at least three of the girls went into teaching. Jessie, Lilian and Muriel took their superior Liverpool education out into the wider world, to make a difference to the lives of children elsewhere. The contrast between their lives, with their freedom, independent income, and opportunity to learn and explore the world, could not have contrasted more sharply with the life of their mother, Ellen. On all the available census returns, no occupation is ever listed for her – she was born in 1843, a time when opportunities for women to experience higher education or join the professions were a great deal more limited. However, this is not to decry Ellen's life. She may well have been completely content to be a wife, mother and homemaker, and to watch with pride as her daughters achieved what she almost certainly could have done, had she had similar opportunities.

Reformatories

In the nineteenth century, social activists and reformers worked towards special provision for troubled and vulnerable children well into their teenage years. Following the Youthful Offenders Act, 1854, courts had the authority to send any person under the age of 16 to a reformatory school at the end of any prison sentence lasting for longer than fourteen days. Under the auspices of the Liverpool Reformatory Association, two girls' reformatories were set up, Mount Vernon Green (1857–1916), and Toxteth Park based at 9, Parkhill Road (1855–1921). Girls who misbehaved and broke the law suffered greater levels of disapproval and condemnation than males, especially girls who were regarded as immoral, had a sexual history, sexually transmitted diseases, and/or an illegitimate child. At the time, it was thought that criminal tendencies could be inherited. An Inspector who visited the girls' reformatory at Mount Vernon gloomily reported:

> The girls are taken from a class which is familiar with criminal practice and immoral living.... During the past year there have been outbreaks of evil tendency and inclination reverting to acts of theft, lying, disobedience, rudeness and impropriety. The inmates seem to be drawn from a still lower stratum than ever before and are very unpromising materials. To raise such a class from the depth of depravity and utter neglect ... is indeed a work of Christian charity.

Life in the reformatories was designed to be hard, but fair. Discipline was physical – the birch was used until 1915, when it was replaced by the cane. Until the twentieth century, other punishments included having one's hair cut off, and solitary confinement for days at a time, with only bread and water as sustenance. The Toxteth Park reformatory was known to be the more unruly of the two, with issues around absconding, laziness, insolence, and highly disruptive disturbances – as early as the 1860s, a Miss Elizabeth Molleson, originally from Glasgow, was appointed as the superintendent, because of her reputation for toughness, to restore order to the reformatory. In 1871, she was in charge of Mount Vernon reformatory, with a residential staff of three, and seventy-three inmates – one girl was aged 11, two were 19, but most were aged 16 to 18. Twenty-eight of the girls were born in Liverpool, but the rest came from all over the country – Kent, London, other towns in Lancashire and Cheshire, Surrey, the Midlands, and Norfolk, as examples. Liverpool reformatories were regarded as exemplars of their type, and authorities all over the country were eager to send girls to them, to be reformed and transformed as far as possible into respectable citizens who could hold down a job as a domestic servant and keep out of trouble.

The girls had all broken the law, and most were petty thieves. In 1894, Elizabeth, aged 15, was sentenced to 3½ years for begging in Lime Street. The following year, Margaret, also aged 15, stole a shirt and two shillings from her mother – she received a four-year sentence. Some crimes were not petty – also in 1895, 13-year-old Beatrice, from Great Yarmouth in Norfolk, was sentenced to five years' imprisonment for 'administering the poison spirits of salts to her mother with intent to injure'. In 1920, Irene, aged 15, was sentenced to three years for theft of a bunch of flowers. Each new inmate arrived at the reformatory with police escort.

Dormitories were cramped, with very little space between the beds. This encouraged the spread of infectious illnesses, which affected the reformatories from time to time – scarlatina, smallpox, tuberculosis, and diphtheria. Each reformatory had a school room and schoolmistress, and the girls should have had about fifteen hours formal education a week, but inspectors' reports reveal that other tasks, such as the commercial laundry activities, regularly ate into school time. Every day, the girls had scripture instruction and bible readings, prayers, and hymns.

Religious instruction was given on Mondays, Thursday, and Fridays, and occasional temperance lectures. Physical education – drilling to music – was compulsory, using bar bells and dumb bells. Deportment was a surprising part of the curriculum, until one reads that '…upright carriage and a graceful manner of walking are valuable assets to a girl going into service' – in other words, she made a better servant if she stood upright. Rather more pleasant was the two-hour walk outside the school premises, held each Saturday, plus an hour's play in the garden each day.

The girls had to make their own uniform – a calico skirt, high-necked, long-sleeved blouse, apron, linen bonnet, and knitted stockings; they also did all the domestic work.

Much of the revenue at Mount Vernon came from the commercial laundry, in which the girls worked long and hard. Consignments of laundry were taken from the boys' reformatory ships, private families, nursing homes, and the occasional hotel. It was a deeply unpleasant environment, with little or no concession to safety for these young girls. Washing was initially done in large wooden troughs. The floor was often awash with water, causing broken limbs when the girls slipped and fell on the hard floor, and oppressively hot and humid to the point where it caused lung and joint problems. The extremely hot water caused scalds and burns – one girl received such a serious scalding from falling into a trough of hot water that she died the next day. If they did not receive water burns, at the very least the girls had damaged hands, with the skin peeling off from constant immersion in hot soapy water. The drying room had two coke-fuelled fires and was also extremely hot; once the items were dry, the laundry was passed to the ironing girls. The large stove where the flat irons were kept hot gave off such a dangerously fierce blast of heat that it ruined complexions and made the faces of these young girls look weathered and old. Eventually, a special screen had to be erected to protect the girls from its effects. Finally, any mending was done, and the laundry packed up ready to be returned to the customers – trusted girls would be sent out with the laundry cart to deliver the parcels to private homes. Customers were fussy, especially the fashionable ladies who wanted their highly detailed, pin-tucked, and frilled undergarments mended and ironed to perfection, and complaints about the quality of the work were not uncommon.

The female staff worked hard to rehabilitate the girls, often at great cost to their own physical and mental wellbeing. The turnover of staff was frequent, something that could unsettle the girls and cause disciplinary incidents. The girls were encouraged to improve their needlework and at Toxteth, they received prizes for their needlework, recitation, and swimming. They could choose books and magazines from the on-site library, although the titles were carefully vetted so that nothing suspect, smutty, or inflammatory made it to the shelves. A course of twenty cookery lessons made a welcome change from cleaning or laundry work. There were other prizes: a silver watch for the most obedient girl, and work boxes for the most industrious. Girls from good homes were allowed out to visit family every six weeks, and there were outings – the Walker Gallery, and Mander's Menagerie. Affluent well-wishers invited groups of girls to tea parties at their homes, and provided Christmas gifts and food. By the beginning of the twentieth century there was even a two-week summer camp in Heswall on the Wirral.

If, after 2½ years in the reformatory, a girl had proved herself to be hard working and trustworthy, she could be released on licence to a job, usually domestic service. Her employer had to submit monthly reports about the girl's conduct, and if the job ended for any reason the girl had to return to the reformatory. Did the reformatories actually produce sober and hard-working girls of moral soundness? Between 1857 and 1906, only seven former inmates went back to prison, out of a total of 1,213, with a similar picture at Toxteth. Any girl who had married respectably, or been in her work for a consecutive twelve months, could return to receive a ten shillings bonus from the reformatory. The superintendents often wrote quite genuinely about how proud they were of their old girls.

The zeal with which attempts were made to reform these girls extended to religious organisations too. The Church Army ran the Parkside School for Girls, opened in 1917 at Poplar Bank, Huyton. It accommodated fifty girls in their mid-teens and in 1920 the superintendent was a Miss Andrews. It became an approved school in 1933, following the Children and Young Persons Act which did away with reformatories in favour of an upgraded system of education and rehabilitation – although it still provided a domestic training (and, more liberally, treatment for sexually transmitted diseases).

Clara, a Church Army worker photographed in 1921 by the Parisian Studios, 27 Church Street. This Anglican organization worked hard to ease suffering and offer rehabilitation in the city.

Workhouse girls who had committed no crime against society other than to be the child of a pauper were sent to industrial schools, such as the one in Kirkdale. Almost always, the girls were trained to enter domestic service. Some of the day pupils at the industrial schools were not from the workhouse, but had widowed or deserted mothers who had to work full time.

CHAPTER FIVE

Mixing With the Woollybacks: Liverpool Women and Leisure

(*Woollyback: a person from outside Liverpool most often used to describe non-Liverpudlians from Lancashire, Cheshire and North Wales*)

The moon is sailing high and bright
And Bold Street is a sea of light,
But brighter still the music hall,
Light streams from every window tall.

(Extract from *Bold Street*, a poem in the anthology *Rhymes of Old Liverpool* by Eveline B. Saxton)

Excursions

For many working-class women and girls, the best they could hope for was an afternoon off at the local park, of which there were many in Liverpool following an initiative in 1868 to provide and improve outdoor public spaces. Sefton, Newsham and Stanley parks alone cost the city £670,000, and by c.1900 the public spaces amounted to 1,000 acres. Prince's Park was closest to the city centre and thus handy for those working and living there. It could be approached by Prince's Road, a boulevard style avenue, or by Catherine Street or Upper Parliament Street. Within its nearly forty-five acres, Prince's Park had a lake, flowerbeds, and ample opportunity for promenading – strolling around, to see and be seen. Stanley Park had an aviary, while Sefton Park had the popular palm house constructed in 1896.

For those with spending money, excursions were extremely popular. Sub-rural villages such as Childwall were popular with

The palm house, one of many attractive features at Sefton Park, c.1906. Liverpool's green spaces and parks were safe places for females to visit, socialise, and even do some courting!

visitors and relatively cheap to get to, especially after the bicycling craze took hold in the last quarter of the nineteenth century. The Wirral was an ever-popular destination. On Saturday, 27 August 1853, the 'gala day of the manufacturing people' in and around Liverpool, Nathaniel Hawthorne was on the steamboat to Rock Ferry, along with a large number of Liverpudlians enjoying a day out. He thought that the men looked small and pale in their dark clothing, but reserved his most scathing remarks for the women, '…so shabbily dressed, with no kind of smartness, no silks, nothing but cotton gowns, and ill looking bonnets…. As to their persons, they generally looked better developed and healthier than the men, but there was a woeful lack of beauty and grace.' Dressed in their thin frocks and bonnets, these hard working women no doubt also carried the signs of fatigue, childbearing, chronic illness and poor nutrition. Little wonder that a man in a privileged position such as Hawthorne felt he could be disparaging.

The ferry terminus, New Brighton, c.1906. The popular Wirral resort was only a short journey across the water for Liverpudlians looking for seaside fun.

Other resorts on the Wirral became the Liverpudlians' favourite seaside destinations – one fine example was New Brighton, developed by a Liverpool entrepreneur in the 1830s as an upmarket resort. It had a beach, promenade, slot machines, fortune teller, and open-air swimming pool. The tower, constructed in 1898 in emulation of Blackpool Tower as a feature and a tourist attraction, housed a ballroom on the ground floor that survived the demolition of the tower in 1919, and the surrounding grounds offered a boating lake, funfair and gardens. For children, the miniature railway was a popular attraction. From the northern suburbs of Liverpool, it was easier to get to Southport for seaside entertainments, or for the affluent, wining and dining in the better hotels.

As early as 1861, special excursion trains to Manchester's Belle Vue Pleasure Gardens departed from Garston at 8.00 a.m., picking up passengers at Speke, Halewood, Ditton, Runcorn,

The beach at New Brighton, the Wirral. In the distance is the tower, opened c.1899 and demolished due to neglect in 1919. The ballroom beneath the tower was retained.

and Sankey Bridge; the return trip was at 10.30 p.m., after the firework display. Other day excursions went to Scarborough, Southport or Harrogate, with children travelling at specially reduced rates. The fare was 2*s* 3*d* for the whole excursion. Charitable organisations provided day trips, such as those to New Brighton paid for by the Lee Jones' League of Welldoers.

For those who could not afford an entirely leisure-based break, pea-picking in the local Lancashire villages, which paid 3*s* 4*d* per hamper, was a useful alternative and still provided a change of scene, with companies such as Hartleys providing bus transport during the 1939–45 war.

The Races

A day at the races appealed to all classes, and Aintree was noted for attracting a spectrum of social levels – the Grand National (originally the Liverpool Grand Steeplechase), was attended by all classes of female society, from elegant merchants' wives to roughly clad women from poor backgrounds, seemingly mixing together without issue. Women made up no more than a quarter of the total attenders, but they were as intent on enjoying themselves as the men were. As today, it was a city-wide holiday, an excuse to take a picnic, have a tipple, and let go of one's inhibitions for the day – it was noted in the mid-nineteenth century that young working-class women were notorious for their rowdy behaviour at Aintree. Some women were not there to have fun, however; they were there to work, as prostitutes. High Shimmin, investigative reporter and proprietor of the *Porcupine*, described the scene:

> Cards have been distributed among the fashionable and sporting gentlemen during the morning, and in imitation of the cards of the horses these ladies' cards have written on them the colours in which their owners will appear … "Matilda, primrose and pale blue", … "Sarah, white and green" … the colours corresponding with the bonnets and dresses. The great event being over, lazy-looking and fashionably-attired men cross the course and … drawing from their pockets the cards they have received in that they more easily distinguish their favourites. The girls, flushed with wine, waited on by bullies and pimps, watched keenly by their keepers, who are hovering about, are thus decorated to captivate the turfites.

One notorious brothel keeper even had his own tent, in which potential 'customers' could find 'young girls and women, their faces daubed with paint … profusely adorned with highly-coloured dresses … drinking, laughing and giggling' with men of all ages from Liverpool's superior families. Shimmin notes with distaste how a young man of impeccable family background might share a drink with one of these prostitutes, 'leering and simpering', yet go home to meet with his mother and sister in the evening without even a blush – in true Victorian patriarchal style, Shimmin spares no sympathy for the sex worker.

There were numerous other race meetings in the nineteenth century within a twenty-mile radius of the city, including Hoylake, Southport, Chester, and Ormskirk. The Croxteth Hunt meeting, which took place at Halewood, had many entertainments to accompany the racing and betting, including archery and shooting stands, a photographic tent, and a band. Some simply wandered around and ogled the 'carriage trade', parked up in a scenic spot to enjoy a lavish picnic. Women gambled freely, just as they did in betting houses in the city centre. In the city, some bookmakers used tobacconists' shops as a front, making casual punts relatively easy to place, despite off-course betting having been made illegal in 1853; other women would have simply visited a street corner where the bookie waited, or sent a family member with her bet.

Summer Holidays

For those who could afford more than a day out, the local newspapers were full of advertisements for holiday accommodation. North Wales, Southport, and Blackpool were particular favourites, offering cottages with 'all modern conveniences', hotels, and seaside apartments. Whole households, including their staff, would pack up and decamp to scenic areas for a month at a time, with father visiting when work commitments allowed. Popular destinations included Colwyn Bay, a purpose-built resort with many hotels, houses and holiday apartments to choose from and only a short walk from the beach; or the more stylish Llandudno, with elegant promenade and hotels overlooking the sea. Anglesey was extremely popular with those seeking a quiet Welsh retreat for the summer.

Advertisements from the early twentieth century reveal that vessels such as the steamer *La Marguerite*, operated by the Liverpool and North Wales Steamship Company, made daily trips from Liverpool to Llandudno, Beaumaris, Bangor, and Menai Bridge, departing at 10.45 a.m. and returning to Liverpool at 7.30 p.m., so that a day trip or a longer stay could be arranged. Fares ranged from 5*s* return for the first class saloon or 3*s* 6*d* for second class for Llandudno (with four hours ashore), while fares to Menai Straits were 6*s* 6*d* and 5*s* 6*d* return. Holidaymakers could also use the North Wales railway, which linked cities such as Liverpool and Manchester with all the resorts and the ferry to Ireland at Holyhead. The Lake District remained a good choice, and of course with the advent of the motor car, motoring holidays, especially popular among young women, could take them across the continent in search of adventure. The Isle of Man became increasingly popular in the twentieth century, as local resorts lost their appeal.

'I'm off for a bevvy!': alcohol, escapism, and leisure

(Bevvy – an alcoholic drink)

The pressure of simply surviving might cause a woman to seek escape, even oblivion in a different way. Alcohol consumption and drunkenness in the third quarter of the nineteenth century had reached epidemic proportions, with an estimated one-fifth of a working-class family's income being spent on alcohol. Women in particular, as homemakers and the decision makers when it came to shopping for supplies, were blamed for this, without any effort to understand why people turned to alcohol for escape or solace. In the Borough of Liverpool in 1858, there were 1,485 public houses – one for every 307 individuals. Drunkenness was a serious problem, and at its height reached a ratio of 1:24 per head of Liverpudlian population. W. Grisewood, in his *Liverpool Mercury* articles on poverty, wrote: 'Chief among the destroyers of home and family happiness and comforts, is drink', and such was the concern among activists at the increasing number of licences being granted to serve alcohol, that in 1874 a Vigilance Committee was set up to campaign for fewer licences to be issued.

Mothers received the greatest condemnation, especially if she took her child into the pub with her. In 1907, the Chief Constable of Liverpool gave evidence to Parliament of women entering public houses with children. At one pub under police observation, over a 59-hour period incorporating different times of day and different days of the week, 1,813 women entered the pub, of whom 4 had babies in arms, and 94 of the women had a total of 99 small children between them. Fourteen children were asked to wait outside by their mother. At another pub, observed for 62 hours over a 5-day period, 1,426 women entered the pub, of whom 7 had babies in arms and 29 had young children; in 13 cases the women were refused drink because they had children with them, so they took the children back outside, told them to wait, and went back in and ordered their 'bevvy'! In the years before the First World War, local magistrates tried to regulate which women could drink, and where, by preventing 'disreputable' women from drinking, and from buying drinks for other people; they also tried to prevent them spending what was seen as an excessive amount of time on licensed premises. However, there were alternatives. In 1920, John Bain, described as a chemist with premises in The Quadrant, Lime Street, was prosecuted for supplying methylated spirits as a beverage contrary to the Spirit Act 1880. The consumption of 'meths' at this time was seen as a specifically female 'vice', and sour comments appeared in the press describing 'many women in one neighbourhood lying drunk' in Liverpool as a result of drinking it (*Dublin Evening Telegraph* 20 May 1920). In order to make it suitable to drink, Bain sold it at a ratio of three parts meths to one part water, and his defence was that he had told his assistants not to serve one women who had a 'dissipated' appearance. Numerous women were observed to have gone into the shop and buy the substance, which Bain was selling for one shilling per bottle – a profit of 300 per cent. He was fined a total of £65 including costs. At least the law was in place to pursue and punish those who tried to exploit the vulnerable.

Leisure Between the Wars

By the inter-war period (1918–1939), the social life of some young women was beginning to change. There was a greater degree of independence compared to their mothers' generation, and the practice of chaperoning had all but disappeared. Working-class young women always worked before marriage, and despite having to hand over their 'board' to their mothers every payday, they had sufficient pocket money and leisure time to enjoy themselves outside the home, despite having chores to do in the house after work. Trips to the cinema were frequent, such as the West Derby Picture House (opened 1927), which by the 1930s had seating for 950 people, or a 'flea pit' such as the cinema in Old Swan; alternatively, for a treat, city-centre cinemas such as the Paramount on London Road (later the Odeon; opened 1934), The Futurist or the Scala offered a more upmarket experience. Middle-class women did not go the cinema nearly as often as their poorer sisters, but then they perhaps did not need the celluloid glamour and escapism of 'the flicks', as their affluent homes were more spacious, private, and more than likely were not crowded with younger siblings who would undoubtedly have got in the way of any adult conversation. They also did not need the fantasy of aspiration that a film could offer working-class women – designer clothes, beautiful homes, professional roles, and so on were already within their reach. Affluent families were more likely to go to the theatre – there were six theatres in Liverpool in 1934, attended by only six per cent of the population. One of the most popular was the Liverpool Playhouse, which cost no more than one shilling to attend at that time.

The cheapest venues for an evening's entertainment were commercial or public dance halls, such as the Grafton Rooms on West Derby Road, and the Rialto. They were extremely popular, despite the middle-class opinion that young women who went there regularly were 'no better than they ought to be', and that the men were 'only after one thing'. Charity dances might be the only time a well-to-do young woman would cross the threshold of the Grafton Rooms, as it was one of only a few establishments that could accommodate a large fundraising dance.

Middle-class women, especially before marriage, had access to a busy and fulfilling social life, but rarely mixed with people outside their own class, and even within the middle classes, there was a hierarchy both in terms of who one mixed with, and what one did. For the most affluent, golf, horse riding (either hacking out at Formby or Aughton, or riding with a hunt such as the Cheshire), badminton and tennis were popular leisure pursuits, as being out in the sunshine and gaining a tan and an aura of fitness was now de rigueur among the middle classes in particular. Club premises were often venues for dances and other social gatherings, and having skills in suitable hobby sports, dancing, games such as bridge and cultural pursuits were appropriate social 'accomplishments'. Young women also attended tea dances or dinner dances at large city hotels such as the Adelphi – here, these smartly dressed young women could socialise with their peer group, and meet young men, in an ambience approved of by their parents. The Embassy Club, formerly the Wellington Rooms where the Liverpool elite mixed, hosted tea dances between 1923 and 1940. At other times, they might motor out to Southport with their boyfriends to the Prince of Wales Hotel, which laid on popular and upmarket dinner dances for the Merseyside elite. Restaurants such as the Bear's Paw also held dinner dances. Most spectacular, no doubt, would be the gatherings held on a Cunard liner, which could be hired for the evening for lavish charitable events. Many of these functions carried on regardless of the inter-war depression, these privileged young women shielded from the privations and worries it caused.

Out in the Fresh Air

Although getting out into the countryside might seem like a cheap way to enjoy oneself and keep fit at the same time, in fact, rambling, hiking and youth-hostelling tended to be reserved for the ones who could afford the equipment, clothing and club subscriptions that went with it – although many of those from lower middle-class and aspirant working-class families would save hard to get what they needed to enjoy the outdoors. The Youth Hostels Association was founded in 1930, and became a very popular way of getting out into the wilds – by 1937 there

Young Liverpool woman posing outside a tent on a weekend away, camping. Possibly the Wirral or North Wales. For those who could afford the equipment and the leisure time, such outdoor activities were increasingly popular after the First World War.

were 275 hostels nationwide, being used by 70,505 members. Groups of friends would set out on their walking holiday, and on arrival at the hostel would be segregated into female and male only dormitories. In the morning everyone had to help with the daily chores before leaving for that day's walking or climbing. North Wales, the Lake District, and the Wirral were all popular destinations for Liverpudlians who could afford the time and funds for outdoor pursuits.

A luxurious way to enjoy the countryside was motoring, with the 'run in the country' becoming an increasingly popular pastime. By 1939, there were 2 million cars on the nation's roads, and well-off young women would join a group of friends at a roadhouse on the Fylde coast, stopping for lunch or an evening dinner and dance. A roadhouse was just a country pub that was too out of the way to be frequented by anyone who did not have a car, and so one could be assured of only meeting one's social peers there. While it may seem little more than a question of semantics to the modern reader, a clear distinction was made between these eateries and the local pub, as it was not considered acceptable for women of any class or age to be seen frequenting a pub, especially alone. Visits to scenic spots outside the Liverpool area were to come largely to an abrupt halt with the outbreak of the Second World War, until the post-war period when the growth of leisure travel resumed.

The most respectable place to socialise was a church function or club, and women from all parts of Liverpool society enjoyed the social benefits that a place of worship could offer. For single young women, in the vast majority of denominations, youth clubs, dances, and outings all offered opportunities to mix with one's peers of both genders, with the approval of parents or spouses. Debating clubs were popular, offering opportunities to socialise and build confidence. The friendships made in young adulthood often stayed with women for a lifetime, with fond memories of social gatherings at home with close friends with dancing and group games (more prevalent in middle-class families who had the space to host such a party), or if this was too ambitious, simply having one's best friend to tea could be a real treat.

Leisure Time at Home

How did Liverpool's women entertain themselves at home if it was not possible to go out? It was perhaps easier to be at leisure in a spacious, warm and well-furnished affluent home in, say, Allerton, than in a working-class house. However, all women could perfect a handicraft such as sewing, and with the advent in 1912 of the first commercial knitting pattern, knitting became both fashionable and practical. Embroidering household linens was a popular choice, especially for a young woman building her 'bottom drawer' of items ready for marriage. Rug-making, tatting, and crochet featured heavily in the 'make it yourself' articles in women's magazines. Working-class women were more likely to make their own clothes, out of necessity, and homemade accessories were a popular gift. Card and board games were popular, involving visiting friends and family. Libraries provided leisure reading, but social classes obtained their books from different sources. A middle-class woman would patronise a private circulating library such as Boots Book-Lovers' or W. H. Smiths', as public libraries were not seen as 'clean'. The Boots Book-Lovers' Library, which was usually located upstairs from the Boots chemist department, was extremely popular throughout the country, offering their own 'branded' books with content carefully monitored. Ironically, the clientele, so fussy about sharing books with working-class people, were served in the library by lower middle-class and working-class girls who had been recommended to the company by their schools. The assistants were carefully vetted and trained, and encouraged to be well read and knowledgeable about the books they loaned out; also, to be a Boots library assistant was a definite advantage in the marriage market. For those who did not enjoy novel reading, magazines were popular, and for women in clerical roles there was sometimes a 'magazine club' or exchange – if one brought along a magazine to donate to the club, you could borrow a different one. For those less squeamish about their fellow borrowers, the public library was popular. Following the Public Libraries Act of 1850, Liverpool quickly took up the challenge of creating a municipal 'readership', with early branches opening in Everton and Toxteth (1853). Loans to hospitals soon followed, and from 1859, sheet music was available to borrow.

By the mid 1920s, the crystal set (later known as the wireless set or radio) was a popular item even in homes of relatively limited income, and listening to radio programmes was another common home pastime. It is testament to how many homes acquired a radio set in the inter-war years that Neville Chamberlain chose to announce the outbreak of war on 3 September 1939 through this medium. The wireless set might share space in the main living room or parlour of the house with a gramophone or record player, always useful for an impromptu party at home. Live music for the lover of classical music could be found at the Philharmonic Hall.

Shopping

Liverpool offered ample shops and department stores from the nineteenth century onwards to satisfy the most avid of shoppers. Bunney's was a staple of the Liverpool retail scene till the 1950s, specialising in the selling of 'oriental goods', decorative items imported from India and China. The city boasted the first ever Woolworth's store in Britain, opened in Church Street in 1909. Blacklers carried nearly a quarter of a million pounds worth of stock. For those who did not enjoy browsing in stores, well before 1900, department stores such as Lewis's would send out lists of goods, and those affluent enough to have a telephone could ring up the store and place their orders for home delivery. Alternatively, for well-off engaged couples or families just arrived in Liverpool, Frisby, Dyke and Co offered the service to 'purchase, sell or furnish your home for YOU'. After 1932, women could buy goods from the new Littlewoods

A busy scene on Ranelagh Street, c.1900, with shoppers and several modes of transport. Liverpool's electric trams began in 1898 in Dingle, and by 1900 would have been a relatively safe way for women to travel around Liverpool.

mail order catalogue, paying small amounts weekly to a local agent (originally it was sent to subscribers to the pools) – often a neighbour or relative. Middle-class families had accounts at their favourite shops so that wives and daughters need not even shop with money in their purses, but simply charge it to their account for father to pay at the end of the month. Working-class women could only shop for basics as the need arose and savings allowed, and tended to keep to local shops, such as those on Park Road in South Liverpool – a trip to one of the better department stores was a treat, and warranted putting on best clothes even if one was only intending to browse.

Sport

Women's sport is not a twentieth-century phenomenon. Those who could afford it took up the new craze of cycling with gusto, as it offered a freedom and opportunity to get away from their locality – often with the opposite sex – that other forms of recreation did not.

There is evidence of a city-wide interest in women's football as early as the 1880s – some England v Scotland games were played on 25 June and 27 June 1881, and in 1920 there was a fundraising game between the Dick Kerr's Ladies team and St Helens Ladies at the Everton ground at Goodison Park. Fifty-three thousand spectators turned up to watch, with another 14,000 turned away due to lack of space, and gate receipts were £3,115; even the Pathe News cameras were present to record the event. The score was 4:0 to the Dick Kerr's Ladies. Women's football continued to gain popularity until 1921, when the Football Association banned female players from its grounds, stating 'the game of football is quite unsuitable for women and ought not to be encouraged.'

Rounders was popular in Liverpool because it had an organisation to support it, while visiting cricket teams would have been a draw to women interested in similar sports.

Cricket was taken up by women in the nineteenth century. In 1890, two professional touring women's cricket teams, known as The Original English Lady Cricketers (OELC), played at Liverpool. Admission prices varied from 6*d*, up to 5*s* for carriages, to allow a spectrum of social classes to enjoy the match at the Athletic Police Ground, and 15,000 people came along to watch. Another match was played on 21 June 1890. There was considerable (male) opposition to the idea of a professional female touring side, but despite this, there were many female amateur teams. The Lancashire Women's Cricket Association was formed in 1933 and the affiliated teams were mostly from educational establishments, such as Liverpool College, Liverpool University, and the Liverpool Physical Training College. Women's cricket also had the advantage of enabling the male and female cricketers at a club to socialise after practice – as the *Liverpool Echo* playfully suggested, 'a match must always precede matrimony, and the church is most easily reached by means of the wicket.' (23 September 1884). Liverpool did not have its own official women's cricket team for some time,

A group of women enjoying a bowls match in Muirhead Gardens, West Derby, mid 1920s. In the inter-war years, more women took up outdoor pursuits, which offered both health benefits and social opportunities.

and in the early days the nearest was Birkdale Ladies (est. 1889), near Southport – but as mentioned above, that does not mean that women and girls never played cricket in Liverpool in the early days, merely that it was unofficial and unrecorded. By 1914 there is reference to the Liverpool Ladies Cricket team.

In 1930, the Women's League of Health and Beauty was founded by Mary Bagot Stack. The weekly 'keep fit' classes soon became a craze, and by the late 1930s the League had 166,000 members, meeting in church halls and other venues around the country to learn the 'Bagot Stack System'. Women wore a 'uniform' of white sleeveless blouse and dark gym knickers and demonstrated their exercises in public demonstrations. Success naturally brought imitators or those who felt they could improve on the original idea. In Liverpool, the League of Health and Grace was established by the English champion gymnast, Jessie Greenwood.

Public celebrations

Liverpool was just as keen as any other British city to put on a show of patriotism for coronations, jubilees, victory parades and the like. School children were given commemorative cups or other gifts – even the girls at the city's reformatories were allowed to join in, with well-behaved girls taken to see Queen Victoria drive past in her carriage on her visit to Liverpool in 1881. The girls were given buns and oranges and a paper Union flag to wave, and were put on a special vantage point for a good view. Some of the girls wept with joy as the queen passed by, so happy were they to be away from the everyday drudgery and at an event that was truly glamorous to them. In 1902, all the reformatory girls received a commemorative cup made by the Doulton works, to celebrate the coronation of King Edward VII. In the early twentieth century, the Bootle May Queen pageant was hugely popular, with mothers and other female relatives working hard to create costumes for those who performed in it. Whether it was a royal visit or a local celebration, Liverpudlians had ample opportunity to get together and enjoy themselves.

Miss Christina McDonald, May Queen for Bootle, 1912. The May Queen celebration was a lavish annual event and for a young girl to be the May Queen was a great honour.

Fashion

The clothes women wore between 1850 and 1950 came from a variety of sources. By the 1850s, the sewing machine had been in production for at least two decades, and by the last quarter of the nineteenth century, they were a common sight in many homes. Clothes might be created by the wearer, commissioned from a dressmaker or tailor, or more frequently, as time went on, bought ready made from a shop. However, despite the use of sewing machines to create clothes, garments for all ages and genders could still be laborious to make, and many trimmings and fastenings were often handmade and applied. Fewer clothes were owned then than would be by most people today, and they were also proportionately more expensive. As a result of the cost of clothes, both in monetary terms and time spent on them, they held their value well on the second hand market, and many poorer people wore clothes that may have had up to five previous owners as items passed down through the secondary market to the most impoverished. Over the decades, technology and machinery created new fabrics – for example, throughout the 1940s, nylon became increasingly popular as a fabric for garments – and this also led to cheaper clothes and even more choice of 'ready mades' in the shops.

The photographs in the following 'Fashion Parade' necessarily depict women who were lucky enough to have at least one outfit that was presentable – even fashionable – poor women often had more pressing uses for their money than a studio portrait! The clothes appear to be a mixture of the homemade and the professional, but they all give hints as to the background, economic and social status, and aspirations of the women depicted. The images are presented chronologically to show the progression of fashion over this 100-year period.

1860s. Studio portrait taken by W. Keith of 25, Hardman Street. This mature lady is wearing a dress supported underneath by a crinoline (possibly a hooped petticoat). Her sleek hair style with centre parting, high neckline, lace cuffs and collar, and layered effect sleeves are also typical of the decade.

c.1874–5. Young woman in the high Victorian fashion. The elaborately decorated dress, with bustle, is typical of the exaggerated styles of the day. The hair style is full and equally ornate, with hair ornaments. Photographed by Daniel Jones of Bold Street.

1880s. Edith Johnson, photographed in 1886 by Medrington, of Bold Street. Edith's close fitting jacket with high collar and slim lace ruffle at the neckline, and hair style with curls styled close to the head make her a fashionable young woman for the date.

122 A HISTORY OF WOMEN'S LIVES IN LIVERPOOL

1885. A similar ensemble, showing the bustle skirt that accompanied the tight fitting jacket. The contrasting velvet front and cuff details and slick, drawn back hair are typical. The bustle shape was achieved with either a horsehair stuffed roll, or linen and metal bands structure, tied to the waist.

c.1885. A striking contrast of the young and mature, the standing woman in her fashionable tight, pointed bodice and draped skirt front is accompanied by an older lady in plain blouse with ruffle detail, simple gathered skirt with modest frill detail and waist apron. A useful reminder that fashion was not compulsory and that practicalities prevailed when it came to age and necessity. Taken by Rattray of Bold Street.

MIXING WITH THE WOOLLYBACKS: LIVERPOOL WOMEN AND LEISURE

1894–5. Young woman dressed for winter in a coat with broad, fur covered lapels and voluminous sleeves. A neat hairstyle and small hat complete a fashionable look. Taken at Barrauds Studio, 92, Bold Street.

c.1895–8. This young mother wears a fashionable ensemble, with curly top-knot of hair and delicate fringe. Her clothes and her baby's attire would be difficult to wash and keep in good order, whoever did the work.

124   A HISTORY OF WOMEN'S LIVES IN LIVERPOOL

1912. A young woman wearing a fashionable hat – this style was often made from soft velvet. Note the wide lapels on the coat, which was probably longer length, to about the knee or slightly longer. A blouse with softly falling 'cravat' style bow completes the ensemble. Photographed by Cottier Cubbin of 175, London Road.

c.1914–15. 'Jessie,' a young woman in practical business style outfit. Note the simple cotton blouse, silk bow, and tapered tweed skirt with elements of the tailoring to it. A fine gold chain descends to a fob watch tucked into her waistband, and her hair is simply styled. Photographed by Lahanc of 145, Walton Road.

April 1920. Dated on the rear, this photograph by Reginald Mobbs of Greenbank Road is of M. Murray, wearing a simple frock with squared neckline, and swept up hair style that soon gave way to the permanent wave as fashion leader.

22 February, 1935. Miss Dora Davenport photographed in her first evening gown, a close fitting style made in crepe de chine cut on the bias. Note the dance shoes with metallic sheen, and her use of cosmetics to complete a look influenced by American movies.

c.1946–7. Three young Liverpool women in their practical business attire. Note the moulded felt hats, simple leather handbags, brogue style shoes and tailored suit. Lower hems are starting to reappear after the restrictions of the war.

CHAPTER SIX

'An extraordinary Diversity of Races': Women on the Move

(Ramsay Muir et al, from *A History of Liverpool*, published 1907)

※

Statistically, what looks like a relatively small part of the city's population came from overseas as British or foreign subjects. Between 1851 and 1901, the percentage rose from 1.4 per cent to 2.2 per cent. This seems almost insignificant, but does not take account of long-standing Liverpool communities that were originally of non-British origin, nor of the comings and goings of a multitude of nationalities associated with a port. This 'floating' population of migrants was drawn to the city by casual labour, and by recreation opportunities while in port. Liverpool's major role in the nineteenth century as a leading British exporting port meant her name was known in all corners of the trading world, and this in turn would have drawn people to her landing stages.

Between 1841 and 1871, the rapid increase in migration into Liverpool and environs led to the development of districts such as West Derby, Crosby, Blundellsands, Garston and Walton. In losing population gradually from the centre of Liverpool and gradually outwards in 'phases' to the better outlying suburbs of each era, Liverpool is in line with all major cities of the times. By the end of the nineteenth century, the growth of Liverpool can only be accounted for by the in-migration of families and

The Landing Stage, Liverpool, c.1900. Here, the RMS 'Ionian' and SS 'Canopic' are anchored, with a crowd of people (including a good percentage of women) on the quayside. Note the City of Dublin Steamship Company advertisement on the building to the left of the photograph.

individuals from beyond the rural areas surrounding the city, and even beyond the region later known as Merseyside.

The Irish Community

Between January and April 1847, 127,850 Irish immigrants arrived at the port of Liverpool, largely because of the crisis caused by the Irish Famine. Some moved on again, perhaps to America, other overseas destinations, or further inland within Britain. Those awaiting passage to America and elsewhere were crammed into lodging houses close to the docks. Of course, a significant number stayed. In 1851, 22.3 per cent (approximately 84,000) of Liverpool's population was born in Ireland, the highest percentage in the country; in fact, Merseyside had one-sixth of the Irish immigrant population, the largest concentration in England and Wales. If you could stand the conditions, passage could be as cheap as 4d on a cattle boat. Engels was disparaging:

> These people having grown up almost without civilisation, accustomed from youth to every sort of privation, rough, intemperate, and improvident, bring all their brutal habits with them among a class of the English population which has, in truth, little inducement to cultivate education and morality.

Engels went on to claim that Irish immigrants did not aspire to be mill hands or factory workers in England, because they would then have to adopt English ways and alter their own habits; even if they did this, some of their old culture would cling to them and it would adversely affect their English co-workers. Local newspapers such as the pro-Orange *Liverpool Herald* joined in the attack, with shocking descriptions of Irish-Catholic dominated districts such as Scotland Road, Whitechapel and the north end of the docks, describing the residents as 'the very dregs of society, steeped to the very lips in all manner of vice'. These are harsh accounts of Irish immigrants, among whom would be honest, devout, hard-working families, struggling on wages derived from semi-skilled and unskilled work. Irish families tended to cluster around the dockland areas, and had more children than some other migrant groups; this combination of poor quality housing, many mouths to feed, and all on a wage paid by the half-day, put a huge strain on the wives and mothers of the community. In the 1851 census there are a number of Irish immigrant families in the streets behind Bold Street with its smart shops – one wonders how the families felt if they ever ventured onto that bustling thoroughfare with its increasing number of plate glass windows and lavish displays, knowing they could afford nothing at all in the shops they lived only yards away from.

Many Irish families were already settling in the vicinity of Scotland Road – in 1851, over a quarter of the enumerated residents were Irish born and had settled there in the previous eight to ten years. Vauxhall remained a popular community for families of Irish descent until the slum clearances of the 1960s. In 1871, forty-two per cent of the Irish immigrant families were headed by dock- or warehouse-workers and living in dockside areas. This reliance on dock work may account for the reputation of the Irish community to be segregated from the rest of the population to a considerable degree, an insularity that was accentuated by a tendency to marry within their own Catholic community. It would also have impacted on their levels of poverty in a more insidious way, as the fluctuations of the weather and supply of raw materials, and delays in shipping, had a knock-on effect on what a family could earn in a day. Of the female Irish heads of households, thirty-four per cent had no occupation. As the city's population grew and its diversity increased, the percentage of Irish born in the city dropped to 6.7 per cent in 1901, but this still left a substantial community of second- and third-generation Irish families. By as early as 1872, a significant number of the 180,000 strong Irish community were affluent or middling, with over 30,000 of them in professional, merchant, or business classes, plus skilled artisans, shopkeepers and so on. This brought complaints from the Catholic church that young women who aspired to better-class jobs were less likely to choose a Catholic husband, and Monsignor Nugent pointed out that poor Irish girls, through their suffering, did more for God than a grand lady with every luxury around her. Another Catholic priest had an equally benevolent view of poor Irish women who hawked goods around the streets, stating proudly '[Irish women] are good girls ... Irish girls don't often go wrong.' (from the *Squalid Liverpool* report of 1883).

Sectarianism

Despite the above well meaning attitude from the benevolent priest, there were women in the Irish community willing to go to extreme lengths to support a cause. Liverpool had a long-standing reputation for conflict between Catholics and Protestants, and neither side can be regarded as blameless victims, leading to activism of a negative kind. Female followers of George Wise, the Orangeman, no doubt whipped up by the riots of 20 June 1909, waited outside a school to harass Catholic children as they left to go home. Father John Fitzgerald, a local priest in Everton, tried to intervene, but one of the women attacked him with a poker. In Toxteth on 5 July 1886, a drunken Elizabeth Molloy, a Roman Catholic, hit her Protestant neighbour, Margaret Sibbell, shouting: 'We'll have Home Rule', after verbally abusing Sibbells' family for some time previously. Sibbell was knocked to the ground, but got up and ran to her house, with her attacker in pursuit. Molloy attacked her again, knocking her to the ground a second time and breaking the victim's rib. Also in July, Roman Catholic woman Mary Gill had her home invaded by a mob, who stole several items and proceeded to kick her and hit her on the forehead with a stone as she tried desperately to protect herself and her children – while her husband hid in the cellar. She was brave enough to give evidence, but was attacked again for doing so.

Despite ongoing prejudice and flashpoints of violence, the Irish community came, and stayed, to become an integral part of the city, and it was a sort of natural justice that the vitriolic *Liverpool Herald* ceased publication in the 1860s.

Welsh and Scottish Incomers

In 1851, 20,262 Welsh-born Liverpudlians made up 5.4 per cent of the population, and the Scottish another 3.7 per cent. Women in these groups tended to have fewer children, and their families were more likely to be working in skilled non-manual and skilled manual jobs, which meant a slightly higher standard of living (although despite being 'clean' work, employment in clerical work at the docks was not well paid and could be precarious). Families of Welsh origin were spread more widely across the city, and were present in more social classes. Retailing and maritime-related activities were present in families near the city centre, while those closer to the docks were in decent housing and the males were working as artisans and in the building trade or small businesses, while any women in work gravitated towards domestic service if marital status allowed. Others still were in the newer suburbs such as Protestant Everton, and working in clerical roles and skilled jobs. In strongly Welsh residential areas, with a strong concentration around the 'Flower' streets off Stanley Road, this community had its own places of worship with services and other gatherings conducted in Welsh, which helped to preserve their Welsh culture and identity, and support their own social life. The number of Welsh-born Liverpudlians at the end of the nineteenth century made up about ten per cent of the city's population.

Scottish families were clustered partly in the newer 'respectable' dockside residential areas of north Liverpool, with jobs in ship building and engineering; however, in the high-class residential suburbs of south Liverpool, some Scottish mercantile and professional families were settled. Those reporting they were born in Scotland on the 1871 census made up four per cent of the local population. The Scottish contingent was centred around a pub called Gregson's Well; many of the Scottish population were Presbyterian.

The Scottish- and Welsh-born elements of the population remained fairly steady, although again the number of people reporting to the enumerator that they were born in these countries did fall slightly between 1851 and 1901 – from 3.7 per cent to 2.5 per cent and from 5.4 per cent to 3 per cent respectively. Despite the relatively small numbers, these two communities tended to stand apart from other communities within the city, and from each other. Lodgers and servants tended to come from the home areas of the household they lived with.

The Jewish Community

Liverpool's Jewish community was first established c.1750, and by the early 1850s, it was the largest provincial Jewish community in Britain. Many more transient Jewish families passed through Liverpool on their way to other nations. Although some Jewish families arrived directly at the port of

Liverpool and stayed, others arrived as a result of crossing the country from Hull, having disembarked there after a sea voyage from the Baltic ports. These migrants passed from Hull, to Leeds and Bradford, Manchester, and thence to Liverpool. For some families, wherever their money ran out, that was where they had to stay, creating a string of Jewish communities across Northern England. A number were told, on arriving at the various cities, that they had reached their destination of New York, and stayed – those who trafficked these families were as unscrupulous then, as they can be today. As a result of this influx, between 1875 and 1914, Liverpool's Jewish population grew from around 3,000 to an approximately 11,000. For those poor families who stepped off the train at Lime Street Station, the obvious course of action was to find the nearest accommodation available as they did not know the place at all, and a concentration of Jewish households developed around the station in Brownlow Hill, Pembroke Place, Crown Street and Coppras Hill. The Jewish community absorbed the migrants, who established themselves as part of their own faith community and as residents of Liverpool. One typical family was the Levys. Rachel and Marks were born in Russia in 1859 and 1858 respectively, and they appear to have begun their family life together in Mela Street. In 1881, Marks is a hawker of pictures, and Rachel has one child, Solomon, aged one. In the 1891 census, Rachel Levy and her husband Marks lived in Mount Vernon Street, adjacent to Lime Street station, with their five children, four older boys, and daughter Sarah, aged two months. Marks is a furniture broker. Their family continued to grow and mature, all educated in Liverpool schools and yet also a part of a strong Jewish community. Rachel seems to have been a home maker first and foremost, as no paid occupation is ever listed for her on the census, but with at least seven pregnancies to contend with, a home to run, and no doubt supporting her husband in his business, she was working hard in any case. By 1911, the family are living comfortably in Kensington in a seven-roomed property and Marks is 'upgraded' to a furniture dealer. They have a gentile domestic servant, and their son Samuel is a school teacher, in 'Elementary schools under Liverpool Education

Committee', following his brother Solomon into the profession. As well as all that their new country could offer, Rachel and her Jewish immigrant and British-born Jewish 'sisters' could access numerous organisations set up within their community. These included a local branch of the Jewish Society for the Protection of Women and Girls, the Hebrew Ladies' Benevolent Society (to aid married women in times of sickness), and for their children, the Jewish Children's Country Holiday Fund was set up after the First World War, to offer the children breaks in North Wales. By the inter-war period, the Jewish community did business in Islington, but resided in areas like Allerton, attending a synagogue on Queen's Drive.

'Just Passing Through'

The *Belfast Telegraph* of 13 February 1882, reported that 300 Russian Jews had arrived in Liverpool on 10 February as part of their journey to America, and, assisted by the Anglo Jewish Association, were on their way to America the next day. Traumatised by their experiences in Russia, the refugees struggled to tell the reporters of the horrors they had experienced, which included various 'outrages' against both single and married Jewish women, and another newspaper report stated 'The appearance of some of the female refugees gave indication of much suffering and privation. The majority of them had babes at the breast.' (*North Wales Chronicle*, 18 February 1882). The Liverpool steamship lines had offered the refugees cheap rates aboard the *Illinois* for their passage to New York. These few hundred people were just a small part of the approximately 4.75 million emigrants who left Liverpool for North America and Australasia, in the second half of the nineteenth century; in total, it is estimated that between 1830 and 1930, over 9 million emigrants passed through Liverpool in order to start a new life in America, Canada or Australia. This is despite the fact that, as the twentieth century dawned, Liverpool was losing out to other emigration ports in terms of numbers, in particular, Southampton. The flow slowed down even more after the USA placed restrictions on immigration, and of course the two world wars created new forms of limited movement; however, transatlantic crossings continued from Liverpool until well after the end of the Second World War.

Some women made a living by accommodating these migrants, who were a part of the city's story for such a short moment in time. The 1881 census shows that in Duke Street, once the elegant and peaceful residences of merchants in the early nineteenth century, there was a large 'Emigrants Home' at number 75, and a 61-year-old widow from Ireland, Caroline Kelly, was the boarding-house keeper. Seemingly, she arrived in or before 1857, as her 24-year-old son, Michael, who was also her assistant, was born in Liverpool – it is tempting to speculate that she was one of many thousands of refugees from the Irish famine. Also resident at the boarding house are two Irish-born domestic servants, Ann Kelly (no relative it seems) and Margaret Gregory. This is a large establishment for only four live-in staff to manage (although there may have been day cleaners and so on), as sleeping at the boarding house on the night of the census are a total of sixty-two boarders, of whom only fourteen were females, ranging in age from 5 to 40, with the males following a similar demographic. None of these emigrants are named, nor is their occupation given, but their place of birth is stated – the women are from either Gothenberg in Sweden (five) and Christiana, Norway (nine).

Of the women and girls who left Liverpool to begin a new life elsewhere, many travelled alone. As well as having to find accommodation for anything from one to ten nights on arrival in Liverpool, they had to protect their belongings wherever they lodged, and be aware of thieves, luggage 'ransom', and bogus officials who would happily take money off the migrant apparently to either obtain necessary paperwork, or in exchange for forged American dollars or other currency. Where affluent travellers were concerned, a simple scam might occur but not enough to leave the traveller penniless – the rest of the scam would happen once they disembarked at their destination, the conners having alerted their 'colleagues' across the ocean to the arrival of the most affluent or gullible, so that they were ready to pose as friends of the relatives they had come to join.

The Chinese

Liverpool has two of the oldest ethnic communities in Europe – the Chinese, and the black. Neither was wholly born out of the best of motives; the Chinese community began from impressed sailors from Shanghai who ran away and hid when their ships came to port, and their district centred around Pitt Street, while the black community had a more mixed beginning. By the early twentieth century there were a significant number of Chinese men with white Liverpudlian wives, which caused unsettlement among some, but others were sanguine about the unions. In 1928, Father Primavesi, the Roman Catholic priest of St Peter's Seel Street, told a journalist 'The Chinese make good husbands ... and the children are intelligent and well cared for.' This was a far cry from the gainsayers who were convinced that the English partners of Chinese men were sex slaves used to a life of indolence.

The Black Community

Despite the fact that the black community was an established feature of Liverpool life by the Victorian era, casual and premeditated racism was to limit life choices of black citizens for generations. In 1850, despite the many nationalities passing through Liverpool, the recent abolition of slavery and its continuation in other countries more than likely influenced the opinions and prejudices of white Liverpudlians. If they could obtain work, many black ex-slaves found themselves trapped in domestic service. Male black sailors were drawn to the port because of the tradition of the Elder Dempster shipping line to employ black sailors, and Brocklebanks also employed black stokers and firemen. However, a life at sea brought additional menace – black sailors who docked in American ports before the abolition of slavery in 1866, were at risk until they left port again, while their wives in Liverpool fretted and worried. Verbal abuse from other ethnic groups began in childhood, often at school, and continued through life. Many public houses refused to serve black people until the 1940s. This was on top of the usual privations faced by any poor family – low income, inadequate housing, and poor wages (as seamen, black men suffered particularly low incomes). In the period immediately after the end of the First World War, a period of unrest and violence against the black community erupted, lasting several weeks. Black employees lost work in Liverpool's old mills and sugar refineries in the period shortly after the First World War, as other employees refused to have them as co-workers. In May 1919, huge mobs attacked black homes in the vicinity of Parliament Street, Stanhope Street and Chester Street; bottles and bricks were thrown through windows regardless of the petrified women inside. The David Lewis hostel for black ratings was ransacked, and individuals were attacked in the street. Some families were removed from their homes, and taken to the bridewell for their safety. Agnes James (who married Henry Brew, see below) gave an interview later in life in which she recalled an attack made on her and a friend at this time, when Agnes was in her early twenties. A gang of mature men shouted abuse at Agnes, then ran towards the girls, but due to the style of dress they wore, the two young women could not run away fast enough. Agnes's friend was the daughter of a vicar and very genteel, but she took action by picking up a brick and hurling it at the ringleader, hitting him on the head. On seeing their leader injured, the other men stopped to attend to him and Agnes and her friend were able to get away in safety.

This was not 'blow for blow' sectarian violence as in the Irish community; this was one-sided violence of a nasty, discriminatory type. Following the Aliens Order of 1920 and the Special Restrictions (Coloured Seamen) Order (the SRO Order) of 1925, black people had to carry documentary proof of identity along with all black seamen in British ports, even if their families had lived in Britain for generations. The trouble rumbled on into the inter-war years, as black Liverpudlians competed for the diminished employment opportunities caused by the international trade slump.

The obvious reason for this hostility to a community that had graced Liverpool for many generations is a straightforward fear of the different. From the mid-nineteenth century to the First World War the number of black settlers in Liverpool rose sharply, so that they had an impact on the districts in which they gathered (an early centre of the black community was around St James's parish church). Employment-based racism such as the fall in the wages of black seamen in response to the 1911 strike by white sailors led to black mariners seeking shore-based work and competing with a different employment demographic (the wages of black seamen fell to £2 10s per month while white sailor's wages rose to £5 per month). In addition, the black community was lively, enterprising and self-supporting, with a strong sense of community, but not one which rejected intermarriage, and there were many black-white marriages in Liverpool. The black community mixed happily with the Irish and European communities, and on a neighbourhood basis, poor wives and mothers supported and helped each other often regardless of colour or creed, sisterhood overcoming most other considerations.

Some women who married black husbands came from more affluent backgrounds. Isabella Stanbury was born in 1880 in Bootle, the daughter of a Liverpudlian estate agent and valuer, and his Manx wife. Isabella, her parents, and her six siblings lived comfortably in Wallasey, and in 1911 Isabella married George Christian, who had an Antiguan father and a Liverpudlian mother. George had his own business, trading in Nigeria and Cameroon, and it was thus a marriage of two people of similar economic backgrounds. The couple met when George was a patient in the Hahnemann Hospital in Hope Street; on the 1911 census, Isabella is one of only three sisters at the hospital, in her case as sister of the male ward. That was on 4 April; on 11 April, Isabella became Mrs George Christian. The couple travelled to Africa together, but their last journey began on 3 January 1923, when they embarked on the SS *Elmina*, bound for Cameroon.

According to the passenger list they were planning to stay permanently in Africa. Tragedy struck almost exactly a year later – George died in Victoria, Cameroon, on 3 January 1924. He left Isabella an estate worth £16,405, and in 1939 Isabella was living in Wallasey with her sister, Alice. Isabella is listed as a voluntary worker (social work), able to help others thanks to her independent means. She died in 1953.

Another mixed-race marriage was that of Harriet Gates, and Bermudan, Edward James. He is listed on the census return as a steward, and Harriet had to find a way to support herself and her children while Edward was at sea. She opened a confectioner's shop – according to the 1901 census, more of a bakery. By 1911, Edward is retired and presumably at home more or less permanently, but Harriet is still a businesswoman – now, with a shop in the category of 'dairy' according to the enumerator. Also living there, apart from five of their children now grown up and working, is Harriet's widowed mother, Sarah Anne, a Mancunian by birth. History was to repeat itself when their son, Albert, married a white girl, Ethel Daisy Vernon Jones, in 1914. Whatever the mix of backgrounds, Liverpudlians are almost always the product of a vibrant, cosmopolitan recipe. Harriet and James's youngest daughter Agnes also married a seaman of African descent, Henry Brew, who in the 1939 Register is recorded as being a fireman on the SS *Cape Howe*. Agnes and Henry named their daughter Harriet, after Agnes's mother.

By the 1930s, the result of this cosmopolitan mixture was evident in the families that author J.B. Priestley witnessed on his visit to Liverpool. In the company of a local vicar, he visited an infants' school, and saw many mixed-race children, the product of marriages between the European Liverpudlians and the many nationalities and colours of skin which had come to the port over the generations. After 1945, black American GI soldiers, stationed at Burtonwood, sometimes married local girls; such 'GI Brides' often emigrated with their husbands to start a new life in his home country. Sadly, not all Liverpool women approved of diversity. One young woman involved with the evacuation of mothers and children in 1939, was scathing about the mixed-race backgrounds of her charges (Mass Observation archive, diarist no. 5397):

> Had hectic two hours shepherding mothers and half caste or half Chinese children.... Felt sorry for the receiving area for district – the mothers and chn [children] are a mixed crowd – black, white, yellow in various degrees, dirty, immoral and quarrelsome and drinking.

On the train, this judgemental young woman had another encounter she did not like:

> 2 of us sat in corridor [of train] eating lunch. Nasty way of feeding but preferable to howling kids and smelly mothers.... Had to nurse dirty baby which smelt. Lorna doused it in scent to try and make it sweeter ... 5.10 Met warmly [at evacuation destination] but think people in billets will be amazed when they find dirty dock women to be their guests.

Other immigrant communities

Other much smaller immigrant communities were the Greeks, Italians (only 500 individuals in 1915), Scandinavians (the Norwegians, often being mariners, lived happily alongside the black community), and Lascar (Asian Indian sub-continent). The Muslim community had its own mosque by the late nineteenth century, at the time, the only formally recognised Muslim institution in England.

CHAPTER SEVEN

'We'll have no wet nellies here!': Activism and Public Life

Charitable Works

Women of all classes played their part in community work. In the early 1850s, there were more than seventy public charities, all needing funds and manpower. In the 1890s, uniformed lady-members of the Food and Betterment Association took nourishing food to poor people suffering from illness, and also offered help as necessary. The Kyrle Society had a branch in Liverpool which attracted women from Liverpool's upper-class families who wanted to contribute to the betterment of the community. Other work undertaken included workhouse visiting, sanitary advisers, social workers, and general support of the poor – visiting families, sewing for families, and volunteer teaching. Organisations such as the Liverpool Central Relief Society sought out those considered to be the 'deserving' poor who had some hope of redemption and betterment, with fundraising events such as balls a popular way to raise one's profile as a charity, and to allow supporters to mix socially with their betters, a rare opportunity for social climbing.

All religious denominations in Liverpool also played their part in supporting women, both from their own community and in the wider population. In 1849, Mrs Levy and Mrs Jacobs set up the Ladies' Benevolent Institution, devoted to providing poor Jewish women with medical aid and general assistance during their confinement. Fundraising included the hosting of a ball or regular occasions, which could raise as much as £600. Another two ladies, Mrs Braham and Miss Jackson, founded six almshouses, expressly for the use of 'aged' spinsters or widows, who also received a stipend of £25 per annum for living expenses. Mr James Braham bequeathed a huge sum – £30,000 – to endow an English lectureship and a readership, also to provide annually a marriage portion to one of the three best girls in the Liverpool Jewish School, although somewhat unfairly, these three girls had to draw lots to determine which girl was to receive the prize. On 15 September 1940, the Merseyside Jewish Women's Effort held an All Star Variety Concert at the Paramount Theatre on London Road, supported by the mayors of Liverpool and Bootle. Entertainment included an impressionist, and several popular singers of the day.

The Church Army, an Anglican movement, had many women in its ranks, including a substantial number from the working class, and the Anglican church was also prominent in the temperance movement.

In 1858, the Roman Catholic Bishop of Liverpool, Alexander Goss (1814–1872), invited the Sisters of the Good Shepherd to open a refuge in Liverpool, their first establishment being in Netherfield Road. What author Thomas Burke in 1910 called: 'the work of reclaiming the sad wreckage of fallen womanhood', was to be the nuns' focus, but sadly reported that sectarian attacks were directed at the 'saintly sisters' property with no regard for the important work and self-sacrifice they were called to do. By November 1861, the nuns had relocated to Mason Street, where they had fifty 'penitents' in their care. Finally, aided by Father Nugent whose efforts in fundraising led to the collection of £3,000, the nuns purchased a site at Ford, and a Miss Rosson contributed £1,000.

Activism in the workplace

Trade unions and other workers' organisations offered women many opportunities to support their 'sisters'. Jeannie Mole (born Harriet Fisher Jones in Warrington, 1841) was a pioneer of socialism and women's rights in Liverpool, and yet she only lived in Liverpool from the age of 38, when she married a fruit merchant named William Keartland Mole in 1879, residing on Bold Street. She was already a socialist, having worked in the London slums, and she fully expected to continue her campaigning, supported by her husband and her son Fred (from her first marriage). Unfortunately, her new middle-class peers disapproved of her activism as inappropriate for her status, although Jeannie saw socialism as being a very broad church to which even the rich could belong.

Jeannie saw herself as standing shoulder to shoulder with working-class women, and wanted them to be more involved in their own liberation from the yoke of capitalist servitude and injustice. Her vision was a unionist movement that welcomed families, and thereby women, with recreational activities and adult education. In the 1880s, Jeannie began a campaign to unionise Liverpool's women workers. In her focus on empowering working women, Jeannie was at odds with the wider feminist movement, which from its largely middle-class perspective, focused on improving the lives of women outside the workplace. In 1886 she founded the Workers' Brotherhood, the first socialist society in Liverpool.

In 1889, the Liverpool Workwomen's Society (LWS) was formed. It was affiliated to the Women's Protective and Provident League, a well-organised group devoted to unionising female workers. Jeannie Mole was secretary for a time, but found her colleagues on the committee less in tune with socialist thinking than she was. It was not enough for her to look to praise decent employers and to encourage a wage for women workers that offered a spartan, if regular, income. Some saw the LWS as a way of keeping those on the lowest wages away from prostitution as a means of supplementing their income. Others hoped the LWS would eventually remove women from the workforce and presumably back to an impossible vision of the saintly homemaker, wife and mother. Jeannie disagreed – she wanted to see strong, independent women workers earning enough to support not just themselves, but a whole household should they need to. She tried to encourage a sense of sisterhood in the organisation, with social events and a library of political and social tracts. Through all this debate, the women that the LWS was there to support seemed to have had little genuine input, and the modest representation of working-class book folders, tailoresses, and cigar makers barely rose. Jeannie's vision of a vibrant and successful working women's trade movement was not to flourish through the LWS.

On 10 June 1890, tailoresses in Liverpool, organised by the Liverpool Tailoresses and Coatmakers Union, went on strike. Many of the 400 women involved worked in cramped and unpleasant tailoring workshops, working very long hours, with virtually non-existent workers' benefits. The *Edinburgh Evening News* reported that the women were calling for a reduction of two hours per day in their work, and 'are very determined, and have the support of the local trade unionists' (16 June 1890). The employers were vehemently opposed to the strike, and tried to discredit the women by claiming they squandered time at work chatting about novels and what pies they planned to have for their lunch! The Liverpool Socialist Society retaliated with a letter to the *Liverpool Mercury* (14 June 1890), pointing out the meagre wage of 14*s* per week received by the tailoresses. The women had widespread support. William Caine MP, who was from a local family, sent supportive messages and a £10 donation for the relief fund, and other well off liberal families donated too. A procession was held to garner public goodwill, and to show the public that the women were respectable and law abiding, even when trying to prevent other tailoresses continuing to go to work. The sophisticated campaign was successful, and the women returned to work on 20 June having achieved the reduction in their hours on the same wages.

Following this action, support for the LWS drifted away, as there were no focused campaigns to attract activism. Following the Trades Union Congress held in Liverpool in 1893, the LWS rebranded itself as the Liverpool Society for the Promotion of Women's Trades Unions (LSPWTU) – with the irrepressible

Jeannie Mole as treasurer. Momentum slowly gathered again – launderesses, sack- and bag-makers, book folders, marine sorters, and upholsterers all had meetings. Again, Jeannie took a holistic view of the welfare of women workers, encouraging campaigns and opening up the society's premises to provide a social and recreational space for them. However, it was difficult to persuade women workers to take seriously the benefits that membership could bring beyond support during a dispute, and it was difficult to unionise trades with fewer women. Once again, Jeannie's strenuous efforts to raise the political awareness of women workers looked set to struggle.

The Women's Industrial Council (WIC), founded 1894, offered Jeannie another opportunity to make a difference to the lives of women workers. It was a bitter winter, with large numbers of unemployed gathering in the streets. Social and political tensions ran high, and there were serious disturbances. Jeannie was honorary secretary, and (Augusta) Eleanor Keeling, a young woman in her early twenties from Walton-on-the-Hill, was recruited to help the cause. Liverpool-born Keeling was a perfect ally for Jeannie, a popular speaker in her own right, and the founder of the Woman's Column in the *Clarion* socialist newspaper, in which she promoted a vision of socialist sisterhood. The women worked together to bring socialist speakers to Liverpool, such as Isabel Tiplady and Rachel Macmillan. Outside funding meant that Keeling could take up the post of paid secretary in January 1896. One early success was in support of industrial action by female ropemakers who were receiving punitive fines from their employer, Jacksons.

Jeannie became ill the same year, and Eleanor became pregnant so had to limit her work; the WIC fell under the more staid influence of women who did not identify as socialists. The inevitable happened and Jeannie, once recovered, clashed with the more conservative members such as Eleanor Rathbone and broke away on her own, while Keeling moved to Scotland with her family – the campaigning partnership was ended. The WIC became more of a social investigating group rather than a militant one, and under the direction of well-born activists like

Eleanor Rathbone, produced a variety of reports – but the glory days that Jeannie Mole strove for, as a representative of poor working women, never came to pass.

Women's involvement in politics

Women also had numerous opportunities to involve themselves in politics beyond the workplace. It was a respectable way to become involved, especially if one's interests were seen to coincide with what were considered to be women's natural attributes, such as nurturing – to take an interest in the needs of mothers and children was seen as admirable.

For socialists, there were numerous local groups to choose from, including the International Labour Party (ILP) and Social Democratic Federation (SDF). The first ILP branches appeared in Liverpool in the 1890s, and Eleanor Keeling and Alice Morrisey were early members. There was a wide variety of activities for members of a local socialist group. Meetings were plentiful and varied, with visits from international socialist leaders, and there were socialist Sunday Schools and a Labour Church. Clubs for cyclists, ramblers, amateur thespians, and a brass band catered for a variety of interests. The Ark, situated behind the Co-op in Kensington, was a hub for many of these, but for anyone who could not attend, newsletters kept members up to date with events. Liverpool's radical tradition was by no means dry and purely academic, but disappointingly, for women, this vibrancy did not translate into leadership opportunities, and some of the men in the socialist movement seemed uncomfortable with female involvement, seeing them more as 'honorary men' than as women who had unique insights and contributions to offer. This perhaps unintentional (men were also conditioned to think a certain way at the time, after all) marginalisation was to benefit the suffrage movement, as there were no restrictions on what women could do in a predominantly female organisation. However, women were able to use their skills as organisers and speakers, and worked on the 'Clarion Women's Van', offering soup to the unemployed. Eleanor Keeling's women's column in the *Clarion* was taken over by Julia Dawson in 1895, continuing to draw attention to issues of relevance to women, notably motherhood, childcare, and education of children. Jeannie Mole also wrote a column for the *Liverpool Labour Chronicle*, along the same lines. 'Cinderella Clubs' were set up, safe spaces where poor children could play and be themselves, and where possible, female members of the ILP were involved – Keeling was instrumental in bringing the idea to Liverpool, but it was not always plain sailing – the children could be disruptive and there was opposition from more conservative factions. Although the WSPU (Women's Social and Political Union) required women to forgo party allegiances and concentrate solely on obtaining the vote until it had been won, many women found ways to support both, so parties like the ILP indirectly benefited from the experience at all levels that women gained from being in the WSPU while still doggedly reserving positions of importance for men. In the years directly before the First World War, however, socialist women were more vociferous in their rejection of their marginalised role, and were furious when the women's column in the joint socialist newspaper *Liverpool Forward* was devoted to recipes rather than woman-centred politics.

The Fabian Society had active women members in Liverpool, but again, their energies were channelled into feminised roles, helping disabled children and supporting needy wives and mothers. Little wonder that women only accounted for less than a fifth of the local membership, and even fewer had positions of note in the local branch, although it did offer women limited opportunities for public speaking.

The Women's Liberal Federation, formed in 1887, offered a genteel forum but still with some links to radical politics in Liverpool at the time. Mrs Lawrencina Holt (b.1846), wife of an affluent cotton broker, presided not only over her own household of twelve servants who tended to Lawrencina, her husband Robert, and their six children (1891 census), but also over Liverpool's first Women's Liberal Associations (WLA). Lawrencina was a sister of Beatrice Webb, a founder of the Fabian Society and prominent social reformer – their mother was Liverpool born. A WLA was soon established in West Derby by Nessie Stewart-Brown, a highly respected liberal activist from a prominent local family, and other branches were set up in Toxteth, Wavertree and Birkenhead. Many of the members who joined her association and others were also actively involved in social campaigns beyond the Liberal party, including the suffrage campaign. Despite some paternalistic tolerance of women's activism in the Liberal Party, so long as it didn't go too far and was confined to issues affecting women and the family, the party offered more freedom of involvement than the Conservative Primrose League. Membership of a WLA could be a springboard into public life, such as membership of a local Board of Guardians, working as a sanitary inspector, or inspecting lodging houses, although this again reflects the view at the time that women must be seen to use their feminine skills of nurturing and caring if they chose to enter public life. However, many Liberal women shied away from standing in local elections, not helped by the ambivalence of their male colleagues. Eleanor Rathbone was a successful and notable exception, and her female party colleagues worked hard for her election to the council in 1910. She was the city's first female councillor, elected only two years after women were first permitted to stand for election as councillors, and she held the post for twenty-five years. It was she who put a pro-suffrage resolution before the council, which was passed with a large majority.

The female membership of the Liverpool Primrose league was influential in obtaining a Conservative victory in the city council elections of 1895, even though males were in the majority in the League as a whole. The League had had women members since 1884, and Toxteth in particular had a lively female membership of over 1,000. Most members were wealthy, educated women, confident in their status – the Toxteth branch was chaired by Baroness de Worms and another prominent Liverpool member was Mrs Brocklebank. There was some relaxation – in 1902, women from the Waterloo branch (known as a 'habitation') established a cycling group and cycled into the countryside several times a week.

Women in Office

Liverpool's first woman mayor was Margaret Beavan (1877–1931), 'the little mother of Liverpool.' She believed that a mayor should make everybody feel that they had a stake in community life, whatever their age or religion. Born and educated in Liverpool, she worked hard for and with children's hospitals. Nationally, she was vice president of the National Association of Maternity and Child Welfare and a member of the National Council of Women of Great Britain, but was also connected with another great civic achievement – in April 1928, it was she who shook hands with the Mayor of Birkenhead when the two pilot tunnels met under the River Mersey, wearing her oilskins and gumboots, every inch the business-like and hands-on political leader. She developed pneumonia and died on 21 February 1931, so never saw the grand opening of the tunnel in 1934, which linked Liverpool and the Wirral forever and brought both sides firmly into the age of the car. Now it was even easier for affluent workers to live on the Wirral and commute to Liverpool, and for anyone with access to a car to travel either way for leisure, at a time of their choosing.

A formidable mother and daughter had a significant influence not just on Liverpool, but in the case of the daughter, on national affairs also. Mary Hardie Bamber (née Little) – 'Ma Bamber' – was born in Linlithgow, Scotland, in 1874, and enjoyed an early life of privilege and private education until her father, an alcoholic, abandoned the family. Their fortunes changed dramatically, and Mary's mother, Agnes, had to take cleaning work in an attempt to keep the family together. The family moved to Liverpool when Mary's older brother David secured a job there as a printer's compositor; in 1891, they were living in Sutherland Street, West Derby, a family of five plus a boarder, and Mary was working as an apprentice bookbinder. Towards the end of 1898, Mary married another bookbinder, Hugh Bamber, and in 1901, they were living at Zante Street in Everton, with their baby daughter, plus Agnes and Mary's brother, Hugh. That baby daughter was to grow up to be as passionate a campaigner as her mother.

Mary became an indefatigable campaigner. In the bitter winter of 1906, she was part of a team of women making soup to sell for a farthing a bowl by St George's Hall on Lime Street. Her house was always open to visiting socialists, and she visited the sick and collected money for the unemployed. She was a fine public speaker, praised by Sylvia Pankhurst for her ability to rouse an audience, and despised sectarianism in Liverpool, regularly heckling at political rallies be they Catholic or Protestant. As her daughter grew up, Mary was a worker for the Warehouse Worker's Union, encouraging women from local factories to organise and fight for better pay and conditions. Mary was present at the 'Bloody Sunday' demonstration during the 1911 general transport strike, when workers were killed and injured at a rally, but it was 1919 that would be a momentous year for her. She stood as the Labour council candidate in Everton, campaigning on issues such as municipal laundries and education, and won by a tiny majority; also in that year, Mary was a founder member of the local Communist Party, travelling to Moscow the following year to attend the Second Congress of the Third International. She was a local committee member on the National Unemployed Workers Committee and, in September 1921, was one of those arrested at the occupation of the Walker Art Gallery. Mary was a true activist, however, and came to feel that her work as a councillor and a member of the Communist Party were impeding her freedom. She left the Communist Party a few years later, and did not seek re-election as a councillor, but continued to demonstrate tirelessly for causes she passionately believed in. Mary died in 1938.

Mary's daughter, Margaret Elizabeth 'Bessie' Braddock (1899–1970), was an ebullient character, who attended her first political meeting as a babe in arms with her mother. As a child she accompanied her mother on the streets as Mary tried to help the unemployed and the hungry, recalling years later the 'blank, hopeless stares, day after day, week after week', of those desperately struggling to survive. She, too, was a member of the Communist Party but left in favour of the Labour Party in 1922. Bessie became a councillor for the St Anne's ward in 1930, and was a passionate campaigner against poverty and poor living conditions, once taking a 2ft megaphone into the council chamber to make a point! Her husband, Jack, was also a Labour politician and became leader of the city council. Bessie took a pragmatic approach to issues affecting women and children, rather than an ideologically feminist one. She chaired the Maternity and Child Welfare sub-committee from 1934, which was responsible for opening a Maternity and Child Welfare Centre in Everton, the only one of its kind in the country at the time. Almost immediately, Bessie organised a non-partisan national conference on Maternity and Child Welfare. The conference called for improved pre- and post-natal care, and for birth control clinics to be set up in all health authorities, an issue she felt strongly about. It was also a subject that put her at odds with the local Labour leadership, a conflict of opinion that became bitter when, in 1936, the leader of the Labour Party group tried to prevent a grant being renewed to a local clinic where birth control was promoted. In defence of contraception, Bessie suggested that seventy-five per cent of the eighty-seven women who had died in childbirth the previous year might have been alive if they had had access to birth control. Thankfully, Bessie and her like-minded colleagues prevailed, and won the vote, despite there being a large number of Labour councillors who were Roman Catholic, and voted against the continuation of funding. 'Battling Bessie' became the Labour MP for Liverpool Exchange (formerly Conservative) in 1945, with a majority of 665. She was the first local female Member of Parliament. At the 1951 election, her majority rose to 6,835, and she held the seat until 1970.

The Vote

By the nineteenth century, the division between home and the outside world seemed like a chasm, and many educated, middle-class women felt detached from public life. It was not enough to influence events through their menfolk – they wanted to make a difference in their own right. The arguments against were many, from the bizarre to the vindictive – women did not have a 'head' for politics; they were not intelligent enough; they should concentrate on their husband and home and mind their own business; and in Liverpool, even sectarianism played a part. At one point, it was suggested that campaigners for women's suffrage were in league with the Wiseites (followers of George Wise, the campaigning Orangeman) to liberate Catholic nuns from their 'enslavement'.

In 1866, a number of local women, including Josephine Butler, were among the 1,499 signatories to the Women's Suffrage Petition. Butler worked passionately for the suffrage cause, collecting hundreds of signatures for a later petition presented to Parliament by William Rathbone in 1869, and another one was presented to Parliament in 1870. She continued her campaign by founding the first local organisation for the cause in 1871, the Liverpool National Society for Promoting Women's Suffrage. She believed strongly that proper work training and education for females would make the case for votes for women even stronger. The campaign was no doubt encouraged by the 1869 Municipal Corporations Franchise Act, which bestowed the vote on some women ratepayers in local elections – in Liverpool, this meant 8,398 women received a local vote, and campaigners held a celebratory meeting at Hope Hall with leading campaigner, Lydia Becker, as speaker.

The early suffrage campaign was dominated in Liverpool by women of status, with affiliations to liberal or conservative politics. Having already gained experience of social activism and philanthropy and with the support of their husbands and families, they were well placed to take up the cause of votes for women, and their social connections meant they may well end up working with established friends; their superior education and the fact that they could devote much of their time to causes as they did not need to work, also gave them an advantage over working-class women, who often didn't have the education, experience, energy or time to devote to causes, especially once they married. Nessie Stewart-Brown and Edith Bright, both Liberals, were prominent activists in this rather genteel world of the middle-class reformers. The 'respectable' nature of the campaign at this time is indicated by Edith Bright's parallel involvement in the Mothers' Union (an Anglican association) and the Women's Liberal Federation. Both women also had an interest in the unionisation of women workers, but believed that giving women the vote would be a vital step towards improving women's lives in other areas. Edith Bright went a step further, and in 1894, was instrumental in the foundation of the local branch of the Liverpool Women's Suffrage Society (LWSS), although it was absorbed into the NUWSS (National Union of Women's Suffrage Societies) on its formation in 1897.

The Conservative and Unionist Women's Franchise Association was a hub for women who were members of the Conservative party, and it was active by 1910. While its party allegiance might have been a restriction, it did offer the women who joined a grounding in political campaigning, but within a limited sphere – no public meetings were held, the gatherings instead held in the comfortable homes of the well-off members. The association was hampered by its loyalty to the local Conservatives also, as they dominated local Liverpool politics at the time, and they did not want to be seen to undermine this success. In the end, their campaign was muted as a result.

It comes as no surprise to find Eleanor Rathbone at the centre of the campaign – in 1898, she was appointed secretary of the Liverpool branch of the National Society for Women's Suffrage (NSWS), and also served on the executive committee of the umbrella organisation, the NUWSS. Her future life partner, Elizabeth MacAdam, also joined the NUWSS, as did Frances Ivens, Liverpool's first honorary female consultant. Those who did not serve on committees offered their lavish home spaces for suffrage gatherings, and the whole campaign for some time was eminently 'respectable'. This was a wonderful message to waverers, and, ironically, men who were not sure if their wives and daughters should be 'allowed' to join, but it did restrict the movement to 'preaching to the converted'. Advertising was limited, often only by word of mouth. The local branch of the Women's Social and Political Union (WSPU) was established in 1905, and it offered a more overt form of campaigning to the NUWSS, but at the same time it allowed the NUWSS to continue on its rather genteel path through its branches at Liverpool, Liverpool University, Birkenhead and Wallasey, recruiting women of influence where it could rather than raising the consciousnesses of working-class women. All this suited the likes of Eleanor Rathbone perfectly, as she was one of the many who were adamantly opposed to militant action, and women who had loyalty to the Liberal government were shocked by any attack on the ruling party.

A genteel campaign was not the exclusive domain of the NUWSS, however. Based at the north end of Liverpool in areas such as Aintree, The Women's Freedom League (WFL) was formed in 1907 by a breakaway group from the WSPU, and placed great emphasis on education as a way forward, and the femininity of their members. Their campaign strategy was to target the businessmen of the city, holding meetings in the heart of the business quarter at Exchange Flags, and sending letters to the stock exchange, the local editors of newspapers, and other men of importance. It was not as conservative in its leanings as the LWSS, nor as destructively militant as the WSPU, and therefore attracted women looking for a middle way – many teachers joined its ranks. WFL members were willing to demonstrate physically, however, and in the 1910 election campaign some of them were 'roughed up' as a result. The Votes for Women Fellowship (VFWF) was begun in 1912 by Emmeline Pethick-Lawrence and her husband, and in Liverpool its hub was the art studio of Mary Palethorpe and her sister, Fanny. It was not designed to appeal to a mass audience – meetings consisted of a reading from a piece of literature of relevance to the women's movement, followed by a discussion. Many of the prominent members were also part of the WSPU, but its remit was different – it concentrated on becoming an open door for all suffragists, both female and male, and favoured tactics such as tax resistance and a constitutionalist approach. The fellowship proved to be a useful meeting place for both militants and the more moderate campaigners, the bohemians and the straight-laced middle class.

By May 1914, Phyllis Lovell (see First World War) was a paid organiser for the fellowship, and over the months before the outbreak of war, the fellowship had meetings on Waterloo sands and a cycle corps that went out into nearby villages to spread the word. The idea of a cycle 'corps' sounds exactly the kind of idea that Phyllis Lovell would have had.

Another broad-ranging organisation was formed in 1909 – the Church League for Women's Suffrage (CLWS). Its appeal was limited, accepting Anglican applicants only, but it did welcome both militant and moderate. The league favoured specific roles for women as opposed to equality in every area, suggesting a 'special' place for women in church life, but that did not include membership of the Anglican priesthood. The league did, however, combine what were two important elements for many suffragists: faith and politics, and offered the opportunity to discuss that link, at special services and at public meetings which sometimes attracted several hundred people, and despite its moderate approach, it attracted members who were also part of the WSPU.

The Liverpool branch of the Catholic Women's Suffrage Society (CWSS) was established in 1912, and admitted men and women. It had a somewhat more political remit, as it had an interest in Catholic emancipation. Because of this dual interest, it was one of the few Liverpool groups that maintained a good level of campaigning throughout the First World War. It was founded by Florence Barry, whose father was a merchant residing in Birkenhead – Florence was also a member of the WSPU. It was perhaps this connection that gave the CWSS the impetus to keep the suffrage flag flying throughout the war.

The radical Baptist Pembroke chapel doubled as a venue for many a radical meeting, including some for the suffrage organisation, the WSPU (Women's Social and Political Union). No wonder, since Hattie Mahood, suffragette and member of the International Labour Party, was a deacon there, while Ethel Snowden was a member of the congregation and also preached there; Emma Hillier and Ada Broughton were also active members of the Pembroke.

Just before the outbreak of war in 1914, yet another organisation was formed – the United Suffragists. Their aim was to have broad appeal, welcoming men and women, whether militant suffragists or moderate, or new to the cause. This was a response to the hard-line tactics of the establishment in repressing the militant WSPU, an attempt to keep the campaign going in the face of such powerful opposition. Unfortunately for the US, the Liverpool branch did not form until the war had actually begun (1915), and its activities were significantly affected by the new circumstances.

The 'Wild Women': militant suffragettes

(quote describing an attack by Liverpool suffragettes on the stands at Aintree racecourse. From the *Yorkshire Post and Leeds Intelligencer*, 8 December 1913)

The Liverpool WSPU met with conflict from its inception. As an organisation, it was formed in 1903 in Manchester by women from the ILP, and much of its campaigning was informed by what had been learned in the Labour movement. During the 1906 general election campaign, the WSPU sought a commitment from the Liberal Party to commit to suffrage reform, and their activities quickly marked out the WSPU as very different to previous, genteel groups. Here was a group of women organising and publicly campaigning on their own, unchaperoned, and in a manner that led the Conservative press to refer to them as 'unladylike'.

The WSPU's 'suffragettes' began their direct action at the beginning of 1906. On 9 January, and in conjunction with suffragettes from Manchester, the Liverpool branch persistently interrupted a speech by the Liberal Prime Minister, Sir Henry Campbell-Bannerman, in Sun Hall. The protestors wanted Bannerman to commit to supporting votes for women, a subject he was prevaricating over; at the meeting, banners were held high, and loud heckling was a distraction. The women, who identified as working class, were roughly ejected from the meeting. Conservative suffragists from local campaigns were disgusted at this unseemly display of militancy, but as many of the early members of the local WSPU were recruited from elsewhere, it mattered little. The WSPU membership was partly Labour, some from the radical congregation of the Pembroke Chapel, and also from the 'bohemian' women who followed their own unique lifestyle and networks and refused to conform to the pace and roles society had laid out for them. From this last group came artists such as Ethel Frimstone, Mary Cox Palethorpe, Constance Copeman and Jessica Walker, but yet again, some of these women were of comfortable background – Constance Copeman, born in 1864, was a self-supporting artist, but lived with her widowed mother who was of independent means, and they had two servants to look after them at their seven-roomed home in Bridson Street, while Mary Palethorpe was the daughter of a cotton broker. Patricia Woodlock, who worked incessantly for the new WSPU until 1914, was the daughter of artist David Woodlock and lived with her parents near Sefton Park – no doubt in comfort, as she was never remunerated for her suffrage work.

Buoyed by their socialist principles and bohemian lack of conventionality, the WSPU women started to campaign among working-class women. They held meetings at Copes Tobacco and Crawford's Biscuits, which had a predominantly female workforce, organised gatherings at socialist venues, and encouraged women of all backgrounds to join the cause, although the upper-class women of the LWSS still maintained a distance. Their campaigning was not confined to Liverpool – Alice Morrisey, with her husband, interrupted a Liberal meeting at Belle Vue, Manchester, was arrested and spent a week in Strangeways Gaol in June 1906. In the December, Patricia Woodlock and Emma Hillier were part of a raid on the House of Commons, during which Emma stood on a bench and shouted 'Votes for Women!' until she was pulled down by the police. Patricia strenuously resisted all attempts to remove her, and both women were arrested and found themselves before the magistrates' court. They tried to make the case for women's suffrage by pointing out the poverty and difficult lives women had in the north, but the magistrate was unmoved and issued fines to the women. Patricia refused to pay, saying she would use her money to replace the hat she had lost in the fracas. The 1907 Women's Parliament welcomed delegates from Liverpool and elsewhere, and the women marched on the male-dominated Parliament; Patricia Woodlock was arrested again during a disturbance at the end of the Women's Parliament, and again stated her conviction that she was acting on behalf of poor and downtrodden women who could not take that stand. She was arrested again in London in 1910.

In Liverpool in 1909, the WSPU hosted a huge meeting, accompanied by parades, displays of posters around the city, and special campaign cards left in public places. Woodlock organised meetings at factory gates, in an attempt to draw working-class women to the cause. Events to celebrate the release of activists were held, and more speeches disrupted, such as that of Lloyd George's in Liverpool in 1908. The journal *Votes for Women* began to distribute well in Liverpool, at one point selling 700 copies in less than a week. For those who could get away, there was even a summer campaign arranged in the Isle of Man by the Liverpool suffragettes, understandably so, as the island has close links with Liverpool. In 1910, prior to the General Election, protests were held outside Walton Gaol where suffragettes were being forcibly fed following their hunger strike, while in 1912, a huge gathering was organised with Mrs Pankhurst as speaker at the Hardman Hall. Mary Palethorpe and her sister Fanny had taken part in the window-smashing campaign in London in 1912, and were imprisoned in Holloway as a result.

Between 1912 and 1914, when all action ceased due to the war, violent action proliferated. A school next to Eleanor Rathbone's home in Greenbank Drive was set on fire, and bombs were placed at the stock exchange and the palm house at Sefton Park. The altar and choir stalls at St Anne's church were also set on fire, and pillar boxes were damaged. An arson attempt was made on the partly built new stands at Aintree racecourse, after the builders had left for the day:

> The Suffragettes distributed cotton wool sucked [soaked] in paraffin oil, and bottles of petrol in places where, had

they been ignited, nothing short of the destruction of the valuable property would have ensued. Fortunately, in the course of police rounds a basket was discovered in which was a lighted candle surrounded by an oily substance ... Suffragette literature was found hung on a paddock gate. The Suffragettes also paid attention to the closed grounds of the Liverpool Exhibition at Edge Lane, where considerable damage was done to the scenic railway. Suffragette literature was found on the premises, and an envelope bore the inscription, To Mr Asquith and Mr McKenna, Votes for Women.

(*Yorkshire Post and Leeds Intelligencer*, 8 December 1913)

Far from driving away support, the local WSPU was more popular than ever, and received a steady stream of donations. The authorities were alarmed by the militant action, and anyone associated with the WSPU was at risk of arrest, so to be seen as a supporter, either actively or passively as a donor, became a significant risk. Women of faith had the opportunity to make their mark too – a national campaign to say 'prayers for prisoners' within the movement led to protests at the Lady Chapel in the Anglican Cathedral, whereby the protestors interrupted the set liturgy to say their own prayers. To avoid such 'unseemly' behaviour, seven police officers guarded the chapel during evensong to prevent a repeat of the protest. WSPU members experimented with membership of other parties, such as the ILP or the Fenian Society.

The first salaried organisers of the WSPU were Mary Phillips (1909), Susan Ada Flatman (1909–10), Alice Davies (1910–12; see below, the 1911 census), and Helen Jollie (1912–14). Ada Flatman used her accommodation at Mulgrave Street as a base, and worked hard to build the membership locally – she had no family ties in the area, and was able to commit most of her time to her job and to attending events. Ada decided to add to their public profile and raise funds at the same time by opening a suffrage themed shop in Berry Street, selling scarves, shawls, bags and badges in the campaign colours of purple, white, and green; even tea sets with campaign 'themes', and postcards of their leaders, could be purchased. The shop functioned like many radical bookshops did in the 1970s, a hub for recruitment, discussion, and sisterhood. Ada also suggested that female supporters open up their drawing rooms for meetings to be held out of the cold weather, a puzzling request which would have limited the numbers of attenders – her idea fell on deaf ears, and her colleagues in the campaign continued to enthusiastically hold their well-attended outdoor meetings. Helen Jollie was arrested on 18 July 1913 in Liverpool, but she still helped raise funds for the legal costs of other women who had been imprisoned. Helen's lively approach to her role was popular with local members and she thought up innovative new protests to drive their point home to the public. One evening, she and her supporters attended the Palais de Luxe Picture House, and during the intermission, handed out leaflets about forced feeding, while one of the group made a speech. Even the manager of the picture house bought a copy of *The Suffragette*, and it was reported that numerous members of the audience praised the women for their courage.

Towards the end of 1911, Eleanor Rathbone and Nessie Stewart-Brown set up the Municipal Women's Association (MWA), which aimed to build support for suffrage petitions among women who had the municipal vote – it also seems to have been something of a refuge for those more sedate 'constitutional suffragists' who were unhappy with the increasingly socialist affiliations of the NUWSS. The MWA relaunched itself in 1913 as the Liverpool Women's Citizens' Association (LWCA), with aims that included securing a parliamentary vote by law-abiding means only. The rather exclusive membership was maintained by targeting potential recruits in 'superior artisan or lower middle class' electoral wards.

The 1911 Census

Many women saw the 1911 census return as an opportunity to register their discontent, either by refusing to fill in the form given to them by the enumerator, by hiding so they could not be enumerated, or by defacing the form. Over in Birkenhead, the form for 6 James Street, an eleven-roomed house, gave some details for six persons including Alice Ker and her daughters, and also Alice Davies, described as 'Lady Organiser of the Women's Social and Political Union'. An extraordinary note was written by the registrar on the form:

> The above mentioned Alice Davies rented this house from Dr Alice Ker for a week from Friday 31st March 1911 and it was open for the accommodation of suffragettes on census night, and I am informed, there were 32 females on the premises particulars of whom I am unable to obtain, but which we included in totals on the schedule.

Alice Davies was to be imprisoned in 1912 for participating in the window-smashing campaign in London in the spring of that year, but she was criticised by her Liverpool colleagues for preferring the big-statement protests to what could be mustered in Liverpool as a provincial city. She did organise some big events there however, such as 'The Pageant of Great Women', but she does seem to have had less flair than some others for the grand local gesture, and she was happy to let others take up public-speaking events in her name. It was during her time as organiser that sadly the suffrage shop was closed, in favour of concentrating on new offices in Renshaw Street.

Scotswoman Alice Ker was one of the area's earliest women doctors, and had married a local merchant – she is described on the 1901 census as 'physician and surgeon'. Her indignation and disgust at her political powerlessness, as a woman with a medical career – literally, with the lives of her patients in her hands – must have been a driving force in her participation in the suffrage campaign. Helen Jollie asked Dr Ker to give a talk on 'The Medical Aspects of Women's Suffrage', while her daughter, Margaret Ker, was better known for setting fire to pillar boxes. We may never know who the thirty-two women were, eluding the enumerator in protest at not having a vote, and it is a reasonable conclusion to draw that a significant number of them will have been from Liverpool as well as the Wirral.

Sadly, the firmly Liberal Eleanor Rathbone attracted a more passive and middle-class membership. It is not surprising therefore that Eleanor resigned from the executive committee of the WSPU in 1912 over plans to ally the organisation with the ILP, although she did rejoin in 1914. Ever the activist, Eleanor used her absence from the committee for other projects, including the foundation of Liverpool's first Women's Citizens' Association in 1913. Feeling that the vote was within grasp, she thought women needed preparation for their role as voters and participators in the political process, and sought to engage all women who might be given the vote, including those who had taken no interest in the suffrage movement. However, it could be argued that her sound pragmatism would have taken much longer to achieve its goals without the determined, sometimes fanatical devotion of her radical suffragette sisters.

1918 and beyond

In February 1918, The Representation of the People Bill was passed. This allowed women over the age of 30 and men over the age of 21 to vote. However, female voters had to be married, or be a member of the Local Government Register. In November 1918, the Parliamentary Qualification of Women Act enabled women to stand for parliament. This partial victory was seen by some as a poor reward for all the campaigning, and more to the point, the female population's huge contribution to the war effort. In November 1919, Nancy Astor became the first female MP in the House of Commons. Some campaigners drifted away from the cause in the following years, no doubt especially if they had now had a vote bestowed upon them personally. Now that there was a positive reason to engage in party politics, women such as Edith Bright drifted away from women-oriented causes; the LWCA virtually faded away.

In July 1928, the Representation of the People Act entitled everyone over the age of 21 to vote; the NUWSS, under the moderate leadership of Eleanor Rathbone, had been working towards this end since 1918. It then split, and became the National Council for Equal Citizenship, which focused on other equal rights campaigns, and the Union of Townswomen's Guilds, which worked towards better educational and welfare provision for women. By the inter-war period, the skills and determination perfected by the suffrage campaigners not just in Liverpool, but around the country, were being used in a huge variety of ways to benefit all parts of the political spectrum. As one struggle ended, many more were underway – benefits for mothers and widows, family planning provision, employment rights for married women. The women's movement of the 1960s and 1970s was decades away, but the campaigns of the early twentieth century had laid its foundations.

CHAPTER EIGHT

Postscript: 1945–1950

It was to take years for life to return to any sense of normality after the Second World War, but everywhere there were reminders of what had been. Rationing continued until 1954, and one of the most easily found fabrics for dressmakers was parachute material.

Just as the laissez-faire attitudes towards relationships in the First World War were mirrored by events of the Second World War, so was a rise in the divorce rate. However, during and after the 1939–45 war, the rise was much more dramatic than before. Divorce rates had steadily risen over the inter-war period and by 1939 had reached 8,254. Rates rose steadily over the course of the war, apart from a slight dip in 1941, and finished in 1945 at 15,634. In 1946 it had risen to 29,829, but in 1947, by the time most servicemen and women had been demobbed and were trying to rebuild their relationships, the divorce rate was an astonishing 60,254.

The 1939–45 war had revolutionised the way many people viewed their lives and their relationships, and divorce was becoming less of a stigma, but also they were becoming less tolerant of the idea that all marriages should be adhered to, regardless of how one felt about it. Adoption rates soared, as the sexual freedoms of the war led to an increase in illegitimate births – for many, the blackout had been a wonderful 'cover' with life-changing consequences.

In Liverpool, the slow work of restoring the city to order, and rehousing those displaced by bombing, began. The diverse population of the city continued to cause debate. In 1945, concerns were being raised about the nature of the Chinese community in Liverpool, which since 1939 had increased to about 2,000. Of the Chinese males, 117 had British-born wives – who were threatened with deportation along with their husbands. Marion Lee led the campaign for fairer treatment, arguing: 'We are British women, not foreigners, but we have nothing ahead of us except deportation to a foreign land to which we do not want to go.' These women and their children were struggling to survive without their husbands, with the help of family and charitable handouts; local MP Bessie Braddock took up their cause, only to be told by the Home Office that it would be too embarrassing for the authorities who ordered the recent deporting of some of the Chinese husbands (authorities which included the Immigration Officer for Liverpool) if the decision was overturned and the men allowed back in, although the Home Office eventually concluded that it would be acceptable to allow all 'satisfactory' Chinese seamen married to British women back into the country to take up shore-based employment. Decades later, racial tensions between the police and the black community were cited as triggers for the Toxteth riots of 1981. This diverse, vibrant city was on the one hand welcoming, and on the other, struggling with inclusion.

Some of the old Liverpool businesses that employed many women were still going strong, but were not without their challenges. In 1950, tobacco company Cope Brothers faced a strike lasting three months when they attempted to take on non-unionised labour.

On 5 July, 1948, the National Health Service began. No longer would the medical care a woman received be dependent on her wealth or status, and popular media abounded with images of working-class women queueing for contraceptive advice, and help with eyesight, hearing and chronic health issues that poverty had prevented their addressing previously. The story of Dora Davenport encapsulates the experiences and widening opportunities of some women at this time. Having grown up in the inter-war period, she had never known a time when the vote was denied her; she achieved her first ambition

Dora Davenport, one of the young women who campaigned for the Littlewoods female employees to be given work after being laid off in 1939 on the outbreak of war. Like their suffragette foremothers, these women were determined to be heard.

of becoming a shorthand typist, her hard work encouraged and rewarded by her employer. Like many young people in the interwar period, she went to night school, and learned how to debate and speak publicly, so gaining the confidence to take on the authorities when she lost her job in 1940. After the war, she married a local man, and set up her own business; together, they bought a smart semi-detached house in West Derby. She did well enough to be able to help out her less well off sisters, and her mother. To her great sadness, Dora was unable to have her own children, but was able to adopt twins, thanks to the adoption legislation from 1926 onwards. Her health needs were catered for by the NHS from 1948, to the end of her life in 2003. Dora was the beneficiary of many of the changes her foremothers had fought for. What remained was to make sure that all women, in Liverpool or indeed anywhere in Britain, could take advantage of the same opportunities, protections, and cultural changes as she was able to. Whether or not they did, or were able to, is another story entirely.

Historical Sources

Acts of Parliament

Bath and Wash House Acts, 1846, 1847
Building Act (Liverpool) 1842
Children and Young Persons Act, 1933
Contagious Diseases Acts, 1864, 1666, 1869
County Asylums Act 1845
Education Acts, 1870, 1880, 1904, 1918, 1944
Equal Franchise Act 1928
Family Allowances Act 1948
Habitual Criminals Act 1869
Liverpool Sanatory [sic] Act 1846, 1864
Lunacy Act 1845
Municipal Corporations Franchise Act 1869
Poor Law Amendment Act 1834
Public Health Acts, 1848, 1875
Public Libraries Act 1850
Representation of the People Acts, 1918, 1928
Sex Disqualification (Removal) Act 1919
Spirit Act 1920
Suppression of Betting Houses Act 1853
State Registration of Nurses Act 1919
Unemployed Workmen's Act 1905
Youthful Offenders Act 1854

General Register Office

- Census Enumerators' Returns for 1851, 1861, 1871, 1881, 1891, 1901, 1911

- Census Reports for 1851, 1861, 1871, 1881, 1891, 1901, 1911
- Index to births, marriages and death registration, 1837 onwards.

Emigration and Immigration records

Home Office Records
HO45/24665: Index of Women Arrested, 1906-1914 (compiled for the purposes of amnesty, August 1914)

The National Register, 1939
Newspapers and Journals
Belfast Telegraph
Birmingham Daily Gazette
British Medical Journal
Edinburgh Evening News
English Illustrated Magazine
The Globe
Lancaster Guardian
The Liver
Liverpool Daily Post
Liverpool Echo
Liverpool Evening Express
Liverpool Evening News
Liverpool Forward
Liverpool Mercury
The Nation
Newcastle Journal
North Wales Chronicle
Porcupine
Punch Magazine
Western Daily Press
Yorkshire Post and Leeds Intelligencer

Ephemera
Will's Cigarettes: Air Raid Precautions. Set of cigarette cards depicting scenes of civil defence. Published 1939

Parliamentary Papers

Report from the Select Committee of the House of Lords on Intemperance, Appendix Session, 1878-9, p xxxv

Women's Suffrage Petition, 1866 (Source – parliamentary archives)

Bibliography

Anon, *A History of the Liverpool Jewish Community*, London, Jewish World, 1877

Anon, *Sunlight Household Hints: a useful book of reference and handy guide in domestic matters*, Port Sunlight, Lever Brothers, c. 1884–1900

Aughton, Peter, *Liverpool: a people's history*, Preston, Carnegie Press, (new ed) 2003

Baines, Thomas *The Port and Town of Liverpool, and the harbours, docks, and commerce of the Mersey, in 1859*, London, Longman, 1859

Baldwin, Anne, 'Women Councillors and the Growth of Local Labour', in Anne Baldwin, Chris Ellis et al (eds), *Class, Culture and Community: new perspectives nineteenth and twentieth century British labour history*, Newcastle Upon Tyne, Cambridge Scholars, 2012

Belchem, John, *Before the Windrush: Race Relations in Twentieth-century Liverpool*, Liverpool, University Press, 2014

Belchem, John, *Irish, Catholic and Scouse: the history of the Liverpool Irish, 1800–1939*, Liverpool, University Press, 2007

Benas, Bertram B., *Later Records of the Jews in Liverpool*, Transactions of the Historical Society of Lancashire and Cheshire, Vol. 80, 1928

Black, Clementina (ed.), *Married Women's Work: being the report of an enquiry undertaken by the Women's Industrial Council (Incorporated)*, London, G Bell and Sons, 1915

Braddock, Jack, *The Braddocks*, London, Macdonald, 1963

Branca, Patricia, *Silent Sisterhood: middle class women in the Victorian home*, London, Croom Helm (new ed), 1980

Burke, Thomas, *A Catholic History of Liverpool*, Liverpool, Tinling & Co, 1910

Central Council for Health Education, *Women in Wartime*, London, Central Council for Health Education, c.1939

Costello, Ray, *Black Liverpool: the early history of Britain's oldest black community, 1730–1918*, Liverpool, Picton Press, 2001

Costello, Ray, *Black Tommies: British Soldiers of African Descent in the First World War*, Liverpool, University Press, 2015

Cowman, Krista, *'Mrs Brown is a Man and a Brother!': women in Merseyside's political organisations, 1890–1920*, Liverpool, University Press, 2004

Crowley, Tony, *Scouse: a social and cultural history*, Liverpool, University Press, 2012

Crowley, Tony, *The Liverpool English Dictionary: a record of the language of Liverpool, 1850–2015*, Liverpool, University Press, 2017

Dingle, A.E., *Drink and Working-Class Living Standards in Britain, 1870–1914*, London, The Economic History Review, Vol. 25, No. 4, pp. 608–622, November 1972

Dingwall, Robert, A.M. Rafferty and C. Webster, *An Introduction to the Social History of Nursing*, London, Routledge, 1988

Engels, Friedrich, *The Condition of the Working Class in England in 1844*, (Translated from the German by Florence Kelley), London, David Price, 1891

Garnett, Ron, *Liverpool in the 1930s and The Blitz*, Preston, Palatine Books, 1991

Gee, Robert, *Cholera: a report on the late visitation in Liverpool, read before the medical society*, 20 October 1853, Liverpool, Deighton and Laughton, 1853

Grisewood, W., *The Poor of Liverpool and What it has Done for Them*, a series of articles in the *Liverpool Mercury*, 19 August 1899

Harrison, A., *Women's Industries in Liverpool: an enquiry into the economic effects of legislation regulating the labour of women*, Liverpool, University Press, 1904

Hawthorne, Sophia (ed.), Passages from the English Notebooks of Nathaniel Hawthorne, London, Publisher n/k, 1870

Hocking, Silas K., *Her Benny*, London, Frederick Warne & Co, 1879

Huggins, Mike and J. Mangan, *Disreputable Pleasures: less virtuous Victorians at play*, (Sport in the Global Society), London, Routledge, 2004

Carradog Jones, D. (ed.), *A Social Survey of Merseyside,* 3 vols, Liverpool, University Press, 1934

Lloyd-Jones, Thomas, *Liverpool Old and New*, Wakefield, EP Publishing, 1975

Knowles, Gerald, 'Scouse: the urban dialect of Liverpool', unpublished PhD thesis, University of Leeds, 1973

Lane, Tony, *Liverpool: City of the Sea*, Liverpool, University Press (2 rev ed), 1997

Lawton, Richard, *The Population of Liverpool in the Mid-Nineteenth Century*, Transactions of the Historic Society of Lancashire and Cheshire, Volume 107, The Historic Society of Lancashire and Cheshire, 1955.

Lawton, Richard and W. Robert Lee, *Population and Society in Western European Port Cities, c.1650–1939* Liverpool Studies in European Population, Liverpool, University Press, 2001

Lewis, Margaret, *Edith Pargeter: Ellis Peters* (rev. ed.), Bridgend, Seren Press, 2003

Liverpool City Council (Libraries and Arts Department) and Countyvise Ltd, *Liverpool Women at War: an anthology of personal memories*, Liverpool, Picton Press, 1991

Liverpool Daily Post, 'Squalid Liverpool: by a special commission Liverpool', *Liverpool Daily Post*, 1883

Longmate, Norman, *How We Lived Then: a history of everyday life during the Second World War*, Pimlico, Bournemouth, (rev. ed) 2002

Mcilwee, Michael, *The Gangs of Liverpool*, Preston, Milo Books, 2007

Macilwee, Mick, *The Liverpool Underworld: crime in the city, 1750–1900*, Liverpool, University Press, 2011

A Member of the Committee of the Home and Training School, *The Organisation of Nursing in a Large Town: an account of the Liverpool Nurses' Training School, its foundation, progress, and operation in hospital, district, and private nursing*, Liverpool, A. Holden, London, Longman, 1865

Messenger, Sharon Ann, 'The life-styles of young middle-class women in Liverpool in the 1920s and 1930s', Unpublished Doctoral Thesis, University of Liverpool, 1998

Miller, Anthony, *Poverty Deserved? Relieving the poor in Victorian Liverpool*, Birkenhead, Liver Press, 1988

Morris, Maggi and John Ashton, *The Pool of Life: a public health walk in Liverpool*, Liverpool, Bluecoat Press, (rev. ed) 2007

National Museums (Liverpool), 'Liverpool and Emigration in the 19th and 20th Centuries' (Maritime Archives and Libraries Information sheet 64), Liverpool, Maritime Archives and Libraries, 2008

Neal, Frank, *Sectarian Violence: the Liverpool Experience, 1819-1914: an aspect of Anglo-Irish history*, Manchester, University Press, (new ed), 1990

O'Mara, Pat, *The Autobiography of a Liverpool Irish Slummy*, London, Martin Hopkinson, 1934

Muir, Ramsay, Andrew Geddes, and John Rankin, *A History of Liverpool*, Liverpool, University Press (2 ed), 1907

Parkes, Meg and Sally Sheard, *Nursing in Liverpool Since 1862*, Lancaster, Scotforth Books on behalf of the authors, 2012

Pedersen, Susan, *Eleanor Rathbone and the Politics of Conscience: Society and the Sexes in the Modern World Series*, Yale, University Press, 2004

Pedersen, Susan, *Family, Dependence, and the Origins of the Welfare State: Britain and Frances, 1914–1945*, Cambridge, University Press, 1993

A Physician, *The Greatest of our Social Evils: prostitution as it now exists in London, Liverpool, Manchester, Glasgow, Edinburgh and Dublin; an enquiry into the cause and means of reformation, based on statistical documents*, London, H. Bailliere, 1857

Priestley, J.B., *English Journey*, London, William Heinemann in association with Victor Gollancz Ltd, 1934

Purvis, June, *Women's History: Britain, 1850–1945: an introduction*, London, Routledge, 1997

Rappaport, Helen and Marian Edelman, *Encyclopaedia of Women Social Reformers*, ii, Santa Barbara, ABC-CLIO, 2001

Rathbone, Eleanor F., *How the Casual Labourer Lives: a report of the Liverpool Joint Research Committee on the domestic condition and expenditure on the families of certain Liverpool labourers*, Liverpool, Northern Publishing Company, 1909

Rathbone, Eleanor F., *Report on the Condition of Widows Under the Poor Law in Liverpool,* Liverpool, Lee and Nightingale, 1913

Rathbone, Eleanor F., *The Disinherited Family*, London, Edward Arnold, 1924

Ravetz, Alison, *Council Housing and Culture: the history of a social experiment*, London, Routledge, 2001

Rimmer, Joan, *Training Ships, Girls' Reformatory and Farm School,* Yesterday's Naughty Children Series, Radcliffe, Neil Richardson, N/D

Roberts, Elizabeth, *A Woman's Place: an oral history of working class women, 1890–1940*, London, John Wiley and Sons, new ed, 1995

Rossini, Gill, *A History of Adoption in England and Wales, 1850–1961*, Barnsley, Pen and Sword, 2014

Rossini, Gill, *Same Sex Love: a history and research guide, 1700–1957*, Barnsley, Pen and Sword Ltd, 2017

Rothwell, Catherine, *Liverpool,* Britain in Old Photographs series, Stroud, Sutton Publishing, 1996

Saxton, Eveline B., *Rhymes of Old Liverpool*, Liverpool, Philip, Son and Nephew, 1928

Scott, Peter, *The Making of the Modern British Home: the suburban semi and family life between the wars,* Oxford, University Press, 2013

Shimmin, Hugh, *Liverpool Sketches*, Liverpool, W. Gilling (London, W. Tweedie), 1862

Trench, W.S., *Report of the Health of Liverpool During the Year 1871*, Liverpool, Benson and Holme, 1872

Woodham, Smith Cecil, *Florence Nightingale: 1820–1910*, London, Constable, 1950

Smith, Woodruff D., *Respectability as Moral Map and Public Discourse in the Nineteenth Century,* Routledge Studies in Cultural History, London, Routledge, 2017

Society for the Suppression of Vicious Practices, 'Report of the Annual Meeting', 1858

Threlfall-Sykes, Judy, 'A History of English Women's Cricket, 1880-1939', Unpublished Phd thesis, De Montfort University, 2015

Stych, M.M., *A History of Weirfield School, Taunton*, Taunton, Privately Published, Printed by James Gummow Ltd, Birmingham, ?1973

Tate, Tim, *Girls With Balls: the secret history of women's football*, London, John Blake Publishing Ltd, 2013

Tebbutt, Melanie, *Making Ends Meet: pawnbroking and working class credit*, Leicester, University Press, 1983

Vicinus, Martha and Bea Negaard (eds), *Ever Yours, Florence Nightingale: selected letters*, London, Virago, 1989

Walton, John K., *Lancashire: a social history 1558–1939*, Manchester, University Press, 1987

Wilcox, Alastair, *Living in Liverpool: a collection of sources for family, local and social historians*, Newcastle Upon Tyne, Cambridge Scholars Publishing, 2011

Wilkinson, Colin, *The Streets of Liverpool,* 2 vols, Liverpool, Bluecoat Press, 2011

Wright, Judith, *A Short History of the Boots Booklovers Library*, in Library and Information Group Newsletter, Series 4, no 23, Winter 2011

Websites

Ancestry: www.ancestry.co.uk. Family history research website with huge variety of digitised original resources. Subscription required, but can often be accessed within a public library using the 'Library Edition'. You will need to be a member of that library to take advantage of this. Of particular interest are the Liverpool Roman Catholic parish registers. (Note that there are numerous other subscription based research websites that can also be used)

Commonwealth War Commission: www.cwgc.org. Offers lists of the war dead, both in theatres of war, and civilian.

County Asylums: www.countyasylums.co.uk. Excellent website charting the histories of asylums resulting from the 1845 County Asylums Act.

Ellis Island: www.libertyellisfoundation.org. Search for passengers from Liverpool entering the United States via Ellis Island.

Greenbank House, references to: http://www.greenbank-project.org.uk/wp-content/uploads/2009/12/History-of-Greenbank-Building.pdf

Immigrant ships: www.immigrantships.net. Search for migrants embarking on ships from Liverpool, headed for a variety of international destinations.

Liverpool Archives: https://liverpool.gov.uk/archives. Use the catalogue to explore the listings for this outstanding archive.

Liverpool Museums: www.liverpoolmuseums.org.uk. Access to information about all the city's major museums, including the Merseyside Maritime Museum, International Slavery Museum, and the Museum of Liverpool.

Oxford Dictionary of Biography: www.oxforddnb.com

Vision of Britain: www.visionofbritain.org.uk. Useful and clearly displayed statistics about Liverpool, by subject; census reports; maps.

Workhouses: www.workhouses.org.uk. Comprehensive information about workhouse provision in Liverpool and elsewhere.

Index

Acts of Parliament:
  Buildings Act (Liverpool) 1842, xx
  Children and Young Persons Act 1933, 100
  Contagious Diseases Acts 1864; 1866; 1868, 69–70
  Education Act 1870, 88
  Education Act 1902, 63, 189
  Habitual Criminals Act 1869, 65
  Municipal Corporations Franchise Act 1869, 152
  Parliamentary Qualification of Women Act 1918, 162
  Public Libraries Act 1850, 114
  Registration of Nurses Act 1919, 60
  Representation of the People Act 1918, 162
  Representation of the People Act 1928, 162
  Sanitary Act 1846, 7
  Sex Disqualification (Removal) Act 1918, 62
  Spirit Act 1880, 109
  Unemployed Workmen's Act 1905, 64
  Youthful Offenders Act 1854, 96
Aintree, xviii, 10
Alcohol consumption, 106, 108–109
Allerton, xviii, 113
Anfield, 2

Baby Farming, 65–7
Bamber, Mary Hardie, 149–50
'Basket Women', *see* Hawkers
Beavan, Margaret, 149
Becker, Lydia, 152
Beveridge Report, 17
Braddock, Bessie, 81, 150–1, 165
Bright, Edith, 77, 152–3
Broadgreen, 10
Blundellsands, 127
Butler, Josephine, 30, 70–1, 152

Carradog's Social Survey, 73
Catholic Women's Suffrage Society (CWSS), Liverpool Branch, 155

INDEX 181

Central Relief Society, 1, 27, 141
Charivari/'Rough Music', 68
Children's Minimum Committee, 17
Childwall, xviii, 102
Chinese community, 36, 165
Church Army, 99–100, 142
Church League for Women's Suffrage, 155
Clerical work, 71–4
Clothing, 17–8, 119–26
Conservative and Unionist Women's Franchise Association, 153
Crosby, 127
Cross dressing, 61–2

Dale, Herbert, 6
Davies, Alice, 159, 161
Davies, Dr Mary, 77
District Nursing Service, 25–7
Divorce rate, 164
Duncan, Dr William, 27

Education: 88–101; schools, 90–1; Higher Education, 91–6 see also Reformatories
Engels, Friedrich, xix–xxi, 13, 129
Everton, xvi, xviii, 9, 151
Excursions, 102–105, 107

Fabian Society, 147
Factory work, 45–52
Fallen women, 12, 22, 28, 34–6

Family Endowment Committee, 16
First World War, 36, 63, 71, 74–8, 137, 164
Flatman, Susan Ada, and the suffrage shop, 159–60
Food and Betterment Association, 141

Gambling, 106–7
Gangs, female members of, 65
Garston, 127
Garvey, Annie, 56
Grisewood, W., 1

Hawkers, 1, 12, 33, 54, 68, 133
Hawthorne, Nathaniel, xxi, 29, 103
Hillier, Emma, 155
Holidays, 107–8
Holt, Lawrencina, 147
Hospitals: David Lewis Northern, 24; Lying-in Hospital, 22; Samaritan Hospital for Women, 22; Liverpool Royal Infirmary, 22–3; Poor Law Hospitals, 24; Southern Infirmary, 23, 25; Housing, xx, 5–12

Institutions: workhouses, 12, 19, 23, 28–33, 53, 61, 64, 70–1, 89, 101, 141; lunatic asylums, 12, 32–4, 62 see also Reformatories
International Labour Party (ILP), 146, 155–6

Ireland, migrants from: 11, 24, 128–31; discrimination against, 42–3; in nursing, 24; sectarianism, 130–1

Jewish Community, 71, 132–4, 142
Jollie, Helen, 160
Jones, Agnes, 31–2

Keeling, Eleanor, 145–6
Ker, Alice, 161
Kirkby, 10, 84
Kirkdale, xvi, 101

Ladies Benevolent Institution, 141–2
Liverpool Society for the Promotion of Women's Trades Unions, 144–5
Liverpool Tailoresses and Coatmaker's Union, 144
Liverpool Women's Citizen's Association (LWCA), 160, 162
Liverpool Women's Suffrage Society (LWSS), 152
Liverpool Workwomen's Society, 143–4
Lodging houses, 12
Lovell, Phyllis, 75–7, 155

Macadam, Elizabeth, 37, 153
Mahood, Hattie, 155
Married Women's Work study, 5, 55–6
Mass Observation, 79

Maternity, 20, 22
May Queen, 118–9
Merryweather, Mary, 23–4
Mole, Jeannie, 142–6
Morrisey, Alice, 157

National Health Service, 19, 23, 165
National Society for Promoting Women's Suffrage (Liverpool branch), 152
National Union of Women's Suffrage Societies (NUWSS), 16, 77, 153, 162
New Brighton, 104
Nightingale, Florence, 22, 24–5, 30–2
Nugent, Monseignor, 34–6, 54, 68
Nursing profession, 22–7, 59–61

Old Swan, 2
O'Mara, Pat, 7, 54
Outdoor pursuits, 111–3

Palethorpe, Mary, 154, 157–8
Pembroke Chapel, 155
Pethick-Lawrence, Emmeline, 154
Population; of Liverpool, xvi; percentage from overseas, 127–31
Primrose League, 148

Prostitution, 12, 68–71, 106
Public health, xx, 27–8; epidemics, 19, 21–8; germ theory, 19; infant mortality, 27

'Rack', the, 2
Rankin, John, 9
Rathbone, Eleanor, 15–17, 30, 37–8, 145, 148, 153–4, 158, 160, 162
Rathbone, William, 23, 25, 30, 152
Reformatories, 96–9
Retail, 56–9
'Rituals of Respectability', 3

Scotland, migrants from, 131–2
Scotland Road, xx, 7–8, 129
Scouse: dialect, xxii; recipe, 13
Second World War, 36–7, 79–87, 164
Sefton Park, 2, 102–3, 157
Shimmin, Hugh, 7, 67
Shopping, 83, 115–6,
Social Democratic Federation (SDF), 146
Social Survey of Mereyside, 1–2
Sport, 116–18
Stanley Park, 102
Stewart-Brown, Nessie, 148, 152, 160

Suburbs, stresses of living in, 11

Teaching, 62–3
Toxteth, xvi, 147

United Suffragists, Liverpool Branch, 156

Vauxhall, 9

Wales, migrants from: 11, 41–2, 131–2
Walton, 127
Wavertree, xviii, 10, 148
Waterloo, 148
West Derby, 2, 10, 29, 111
West Dingle, 35
Wilkinson, Catherine 'Kitty', 28
Wilkinson, Ellen, 81, 83
Women's Freedom League, 154
Women's Industrial Council (WIC), 5, 145 *see also* Married Women's Work study
Women's Liberal Federation, 147
Women's Political and Social Union (WSPU), 75, 153–60, 162
Women's Suffrage Petition, 152
Women's War Service Bureau (WWSB), 76
Woodlock, Patricia, 157–8